MY MOTHER
WORKED
AND I
TURNED OUT
OKAY

▲

MY MOTHER WORKED AND I TURNED OUT OKAY

▲

Katherine Wyse Goldman

With an Afterword by Lois Wyse (Her Mother)

Villard Books
New York
1993

Copyright © 1993 by Garret Press, Inc.
All rights reserved under International and Pan-American
Copyright Conventions. Published in the United States by
Villard Books, a division of Random House, Inc.,
New York, and simultaneously in Canada by
Random House of Canada Limited,
Toronto.

Villard Books is a registered trademark of Random House, Inc.

Library of Congress Cataloging-in-Publication Data
Goldman, Katherine Wyse.
My mother worked and I turned out okay / Katherine Wyse Goldman ;
with an afterword by Lois Wyse (her mother).
p.   cm.
ISBN 0–679–41544–0
1. Mothers—United States—Humor.   2. Working mothers—United
States—Anecdotes.   I. Title.
PN6231.M68G65   1993
818'.5402—dc20   92–56814

Manufactured in the United Sates of America on acid-free paper
9   8   7   6   5   4   3   2
First Edition

Book design by Oksana Kushnir

For my mother,
who always promised
I would turn out okay.

And for Henry, Max, and Molly,
who convinced me.

Acknowledgments

For their steady encouragement and optimism, I thank my agents, Jay Acton and Jane Dystel.

For her perceptive comments and sympathetic ear, I thank my editor, Diane Reverand.

For her unwavering support as she lived through it and then had to read about it, I thank my mother, Lois Wyse.

For waiting until I was good and ready to show it to him and for making sense of it all, I thank my husband, Henry Goldman.

And for their kindness in opening their memories, hearts, and souls to me, I thank my generous sources.

Acknowledgments

MY MOTHER
WORKED
AND I
TURNED OUT
OKAY

▲

How I learned
the Twelve Principles of
Working Motherhood.

▲

There are twelve simple principles that, kept in mind for the total number of years you are responsible for the general welfare, happiness, tuitions, and parking tickets of your children, will help ease your overwhelming guilt in getting up every day, leaving your children, and going to work in order to pay for such obligations.

You aren't born knowing them.

They don't teach them in college.

This is the only place to learn them.

You are about to be the beneficiary of the combined self-knowledge of dozens of grown-ups who are the children of working mothers. I join my sources as one who has experienced trial by fire and emerged with little more than rug burns, along with a real understanding of what my mother went through.

The following are just about all you ever need to know. Remember them. You will have a quiz every day for the next forty years or so.

- No child ever fails to recognize Mother when she comes home from work.
- Children who know what their mothers do all day at work are more inclined to tell their mothers what they do all day at school.
- Working mothers are masters at including the kids and making everybody think it was a good idea.
- A working mother will give up a limb for her children. It's just that she has to arrange for time off first.
- The bad news is your mother's not there when you get home from school. The good news is your mother's not there when you get home from school.
- Working mothers do not have to ask Daddy for money. Neither do their children.

- When they want to grow up to be like Mommy, it might be because she's making the best job offer.
- Children of working mothers know the value of working women.
- You can't appreciate her until you've taken a business call while changing a diaper, escaped from a meeting to get to daycare before they lock up, picked up clients in a car filled with Cheerios dust, and felt guilty at high school graduation because you never helped out in the art room even once and you had thirteen years to do it.
- Beyond working motherhood: something happens when you call her Grandma.
- Working mothers develop instant amnesia about how tough it was to raise the kids. It takes the children a bit longer.
- As my mother always says, "Don't get so involved in the duties of your life and your children that you forget the pleasure. Remember why you had children."

It had to start somewhere.

▲

At exactly 4:42 on a grey January day, a woman ran down the hall past my office shouting, "I just came in from the parking lot! It's sleeting, and all the cars are covered with ice!"

Guilt rose up into my throat. My hands went cold. I bit my nails.

Everybody talked about getting into their cars that minute and driving home, but I was the first one out there scraping ice off my door handle with my American Express card. I lived an hour away on a sunny day with no traffic jams or accidents or rubberneckers. Even with four-wheel-drive, I had no idea how long it would take me that night.

My motivating factors were a two-year-old and a six-month-old at home with little faces pressed against the frosted glass, tears streaming down their cheeks, crying, "Mommy, Mommy, please come back to us. Never leave us again!" for eight hours straight. It was all in my head, though real enough for all the agony it caused.

After eighteen minutes, when the defroster had almost melted the ice on my windshield, I drove gingerly to the expressway. "I'll be able to pick up speed on the highway," I thought. "There will be so many cars, the snow won't have a chance to collect."

Sleet, ice, rain, snow; just about every horrible thing that can come from the sky except for locusts was all over the highway. That didn't stop me from trying to make good time. I tried some fair-weather-style weaving, but it was tough to do even in four-wheel-drive. I settled into a lane. My mind's eye saw my children's babysitter in our living room honing a ten-inch French cook's knife in order to murder me for being late. I started to weave again.

Then I saw a gigantic accident, the kind that gets on the news, in the oncoming lanes, just over the median strip.

I started to think about why I was barreling down

that road, why I felt so *guilty* for being late. Naturally, I was out there because I was working—*a working mother.* I felt guilty for doing that. And I was only working *part-time*!

Still, what was going to happen to my children?

Nothing.

I knew I didn't have to feel guilty for not being home. After all, my mother worked, and I turned out okay.

I don't have one of those mothers who call their daughters every night to tell them how horrible they are to leave their children with non-English-speaking women, who explain that the only way to make sure your children turn out okay is to be with them all day long doing flash cards and taking them to museums and ballet classes and baking Plasticene models and *just staying with them no matter how insane it makes you.*

My mother had a career. She's one of those women who gives speeches about being a working mother. She's a role model for other women in business. While I was growing up, people were always sending their children to her for career advice.

And my mother's children turned out great. The way I feel, I was lucky to have a working mother. She was aware of the world in a way that some stay-at-home mothers were not. She supported and encouraged and coached me in ways a mother not in business could never have done.

I lived it. I was there. I know just what it's like to grow up as the child of a working mother. I know it's not a bed of roses. There are times when you're little that you want your mother home. And when you start to grow up, you have a new role model to live up to: your working mother.

But kids aren't irreparably damaged because their mothers work. Guilt doesn't have to be the mothers' overriding feeling. Children are wonderful, adaptable creatures. They love their moms, and they look to their moms to learn how to live. What kids need to see is a mother who's fulfilled and content with herself.

I can't imagine what it would have been like if my mother had stayed home.

My mother started working in the 1940s when she was seventeen. She was a newspaper reporter. She was so good, so ambitious, she was awarded her own column in *The Cleveland Press*. She became a stringer for *Life* magazine when she was just eighteen.

She was still a reporter when she married my father at age twenty; but my father didn't like his job as the advertising director of a company, so they started a newspaper-advertising shopping column. They went around to various companies in Cleveland (tiny ones at the time, like Stouffer's restaurants and Bonne Bell cosmetics) and wrote interesting items about new products or specials. Then Mr. Bell came to my father and said, "If you want to open an advertising agency, I want to be your client."

That was okay with my father, but it didn't sit too well with my mother. She had made him promise never to open his own agency, but they started their new business just months before I was born. When November came around, I popped out of Mom, and she was back at work in ten days writing ads and answering phones.

Family legend has it that they started to do well at running their own business. One reason is that my mother has a tremendous capacity to see the big picture. That's a talent in itself, but she always manages to see it before everyone else does. Since she isn't shy, she always wants to tell others. All of these characteristics plus a smattering of luck make for a successful career in the advertising business. Not until they started working for Smucker's jelly did they begin to get national recognition.

My mother first wrote some pedestrian radio commercials for Smucker's. Then she wrote another that said that Smucker's had to be pretty proud of its product to put their funny name on the jar. "With a name like Smucker's, it has to be good," she wrote.

The Smucker Story is our Big Family Story, the way some families always remember that camping trip in Yosemite or the time little Johnny blew up the basement with his science experiment. This is the story that changed our lives. My mother had written one of those advertising lines that people actually know and remember. Suddenly, she had a very high profile.

About this time I was old enough to understand that my mother did something for a living. I noticed she was different. Nobody else's mother got dressed up in the morning to go to the office. Nobody else's mother had a secretary. The other children's mothers ran in and out of the house to change for tennis lessons or lunch dates. They dropped into school to pick up their children and drive them home. Sure, my mother came to plays, to campaign speeches for president of elementary school, but I wanted my mother home baking cookies and playing jacks with me.

The only times she came home early were to take me for a haircut or new shoes or to the (gulp!) pediatrician. When she got home at night, she brought the office with her. Not work, but the emotions, exasperation, exhaustion. My brother and I would hear the automatic garage door open, scream, "She's home!" then turn off the television and run to our rooms and wait to see what she was like. Good day? Bad day?

When I was in second grade, she told me one very good day that she was going to use me on radio commercials. I was such a good reader, she said, and such an *actress* that she was going to take me to a recording studio to see how I would do in a spot in which I would be a little girl talking to my father about savings and loans. Wow! Nobody else did *that*.

I loved it because my mother was thinking about *me*

when she sat down at her typewriter. My mother turned my precious little-kid words into commercials.

I loved doing it. And I was able to gloat over my sweet victory in the ongoing battle of sibling rivalry.

Until one night when my mother made a secret pact with my brother.

He was feeling left out. He didn't like that we turned up the radio every time Kathy came on. So she wrote *The I-Don't-Want-to-Go-to-Bed Book for Boys,* about a little boy named Robbie who didn't like to go to bed at night, and his mother made him a special nightcap with hands on it that went over his ears and kept out all of the stay-awake noises. I tolerated this, but it became a lot easier when she wrote a companion book for girls.

That was the beginning of another career so successful that she has by now published more than forty books and even hit number one on *The New York Times* bestseller list.

Every time my mother got interested in something, she pursued it. She decided she wanted a little garret at home to write freelance articles for magazines. Of course, she *did* write those articles through the years, ending up with a monthly column in *Good Housekeeping* and now her own syndicated newspaper column. She always wanted to write a novel. She found time to write several, and a couple have even been made into television movies. She wanted to write shows. So she set up a company with a songwriting neighbor, and their collaborative musical was staged in New York, Toronto, and Cleveland.

I learned early that pushing and doing and working can really get you someplace.

Even though she was busy, she made sure we did things together.

When I was young we used to lie on her bed and look at the skinny models in *Vogue* and *Harper's Bazaar*. Whenever we went shopping together, she always asked me which clothes were appropriate for the big presentation or the important board meeting.

Many times she took me on business trips. I went to photography shoots and sat and stared at models making themselves up. I watched television commercials being shot. I listened to jingle recordings. When I was about ten, the agency did advertising for a department store, and my mother kept a little office there. Sometimes during vacations I'd go downtown to the store with her, and she would give me her charge-a-plate and some errands to do. I loved signing, "Kathy Wyse (daughter)." I felt so proud of myself and my mother.

I went off to college and studied literature. After graduating, I thought it sounded romantic to spend my life in the woods and mountains of New England snowshoeing to a reporting job with a tiny newspaper. My mother saw the big picture of life: career and family. She could gauge the future and understood the impact of the women's movement, that women were going to get new opportunities, and she encouraged me to be part of the revolution. So my mother and my college roommate's mother got together and rented an apartment for their daughters in Manhattan, where the mothers both lived. I worked for a year for a publisher, but hated my job and complained to my mother frequently. Her response: "Why don't you come to work at the agency as a copywriter? I'll teach you how to write commercials." I agreed to stay for a year. I stayed for eight. In that time I grew and developed as a writer and spent my twenties discovering myself.

It was fascinating watching her at work. I got to see what she really did at the office. Some people whose mothers work are mystified about what their mothers do. I was lucky; I had a close look at the way she lived when she wasn't with me.

I got to see that Mom was so Mom-like in the way she ran the business. In fact, many in the agency ended up calling her Mom. A lot of them weren't from New York and would come to her for motherly advice. If we were all good and got new business or did well in a presentation, she would take us to the movies and out to dinner.

She was never my direct superior, but she was well aware of what I was up to. I imagined a jab in the solar plexus when she wasn't wild about my work. Conversely, I beamed brighter when she loved what I did.

She gave me all sorts of opportunities. It wasn't until I had my own children, though, that I could understand how she must have felt having me there. I would be so proud to see my son and daughter come into the company I had built and to watch them do well at it.

When I got married I left the agency because my husband took a job in Philadelphia. There I started working for another advertising agency, and I found out how much I had learned from my mother. My confidence was high. My work was good. And I felt very close to my mother.

I called her all the time for career advice. She was fantastic at telling me how to negotiate a salary and how to make an end run to sell ideas that couldn't get up the ladder. I trusted her instincts about which ideas I should push and which I should toss in the trash.

I was promoted to a management position at one agency and was incredibly proud. My career was zooming ahead, and I got pregnant. It hadn't seemed like a big deal to me before I was expecting a baby, but suddenly I didn't know what I was going to do about work. My son was born on a Thursday, and by Monday I thought I was rested enough to go back to work. Good sense prevailed. I stayed home and fell in love.

After four months, I couldn't stay at home all day. My head was mush. My husband encouraged me to work freelance, to find consulting jobs in advertising. That turned out to be the best solution for me. I had something to do for myself, I had my own money, I was able to be with grown-ups, I could talk about more than poopies and chicken pox, and I was able to be with my son—and then my daughter.

Mothers will always be harried, guilty, frazzled, torn, exhausted, exuberant, fulfilled—and if they work, it's multiplied by a zillion. Books and magazines make it sound so scary, as if working mothers are about to tumble into the Grand Canyon without a parachute, it's no wonder these mothers are ripping their cuticles while they wonder how their kids will turn out.

There are plenty of grown-up kids raised by working mothers, plenty of kids like me with children of their own, who can talk about what it's really like so that mothers don't have to speed down slippery highways imagining the worst.

These are the people I set out to find. They came to me through word of mouth, through research networks at the University of Pennsylvania and the University of Michigan, through business contacts, from newspaper articles, and from long sessions poring over *Who's Who of American Women*. I wanted to find out whether children of working mothers turned out okay.

Now, as far as okay goes, it means okay. It doesn't mean that a grown child is extraordinarily brilliant, wealthy, accomplished, famous, or in shape. We all have our quirks. Okay means simply that this grown child lives a life that is pleasing to him or her, that life and its crazy unplanned events are in perspective, that the choices made have led to a life that the person enjoys and, what's more, that the person has become a caring, productive individual whose life means something.

I was intrigued to meet these people. I asked how they did in school, who took care of them when they were little, whether they were proud of their mothers, how often they told their mothers, "I love you," where their fathers stood in the family, what kinds of careers the children chose and how they expected to raise their own children. I listened to what they had to say, tried to figure out what they held back.

None of them had ever been asked these questions before. This was kind of a secret life, but they wanted to talk about it . . . eagerly.

I thought it was time young working mothers listened to grown-ups with good news.

Their wisdom helped me devise the Twelve Principles of Working Motherhood, the main truths that grown children of working mothers have learned.

So if you look closely, you'll find there just could be a silver lining in all this seeming chaos.

And you just never know what it might be.

My mother has always said that her best training for running a business was being a mother.

**No child ever fails
to recognize Mother when
she comes home
from work.**

▲

There is a Universal Guilt Day.

It's the day the maternity leave is over and child care begins.

You might see Mother crying into her steering wheel when she puts the baby in daycare for the first time. Or she may heave a sigh of relief as the kid goes quietly to the babysitter or nanny she had to sell stock to hire. But guaranteed her hands are clammy, her throat is dry, she has no appetite, and she waits all day for the phone call telling her that the little darling is bleeding to death from falling down several flights of stairs or is choking on a penny an acclaimed caregiver dropped into the crib.

All day long the refrain plays in her skull: *I never should have done this. I never should have done this. I never should have done this.*

Oh, go ahead. It gets better, easier. Think about it. The day you first leave your child with a babysitter, you've probably known that baby only eight weeks or three months or six months. Hardly enough time to develop much of a relationship as we grown-ups know it, but certainly enough time to have developed that bond with your child. The baby knows your voice, your smell, your touch, your smile. You can see it in his eyes.

When he gets older, he actually runs to you at the end of the day, calling, "Mommy!" It happens. It really does. Never mind that your two-year-old could possibly scream, as mine did, for sixty eardrum-shattering minutes every day beginning at six P.M. When I asked my pediatrician why my son was perfect for the sitter and difficult for me, he said, "Oh, he only feels comfortable throwing a tantrum in front of you. Consider yourself lucky. If he were punching other kids all day and horrible to the sitter, then you'd know you had a problem."

In any case, he was, and is, happy to see me at the

end of the day. He and my daughter adored Fanny, who took them downtown on the bus and over to her senior center where they got up on the stage and breathed into the microphone. They were crazy about Lillian, who spent hours building Lego ships and castles. They loved to visit her at home on the weekends and deliver cookies they had made.

Did it bother me? Did I think that they loved these women too much, that they would forget their dear old mom?

Of course not.

And that's because I was attached to my own babysitters when I was growing up. Sarah came to my house before I was born and still knew me after I had graduated from college. I used to sit on her lap to eat lunch. I loved the way she smiled. Tessie came to live with us when I was in fifth grade. She taught me a lot about table manners ("Are your elbows going to be on the table when you're invited to the White House?"), about cooking ("Always snip parsley with a pair of scissors"), about life ("Never turn down an invitation to the symphony"), and about garbage disposals ("Chicken bones, banana peels, and olive pits are taboo").

Did I love them so very much? Absolutely. Did I confuse them with my mother? Definitely not.

My mother was the person with whom I identified. She's the one I was proud of, angry at, devoted to. You can't help it. If you have a good mother, she knows how to set it up, whether she's around every afternoon or not.

▲

Beth grew up in New York City. Her mother was an executive and went back to work when Beth was two months old.

"My mother got one nanny who stayed with us until I was six and a half," says Beth. "After that, there was a dynasty of au pair girls. But I loved Nanny. She was about sixty and Norwegian. She read to me endlessly. I did a lot with her. We went grocery shopping, did errands at little shops. I don't remember doing any of this with my mother. I felt very close to Nanny. When I was sick, I wanted her. My mother was not into hard-core nurturing. She didn't make our house homey. She planned the menus, but she had no idea how food got to the table. She was an order-up person.

"But I never felt deprived. I knew she cared. She gave me my sense of self. Through osmosis, I learned I was smart, that I could conduct myself like a person who knew what was what. She was beautiful, but not classically feminine. She came across as a strong person. She was smart and had a lot of opinions. From her I knew I would be a female who does something."

Now, really, do you expect to get that from a baby-sitter?

And are you hiring a babysitter to teach your children values?

A lot of what happens does depend on the kind of person you have taking care of your children.

Rebecca's mother was a teacher, out of the house all of the time Rebecca and her brothers were growing up in Kentucky. Rebecca talks about the kinds of women who cared for her and those whom mothers accept in desperation today.

"In the South, people stay with the family for forty years. They're there so long and are so loyal no one would dare fire them. So the old ladies just sit in the kitchen and sew. When you're all grown and go to visit them, you could still sit and curl up on their laps if you wanted to.

"Today people say, 'God, you've had your sitter for three years. It's so long!' No, it isn't. Mothers need that sense of security. My mother put a lot of pressure on herself as a teacher and a mother. She had to come home every afternoon and play solitaire for an hour to calm down. She wasn't there to listen to the kids. Can you imagine if we didn't have someone competent there? My mother was good at getting people like her to take care of the kids.

"One of my neighbors is a lawyer who's never home. She has a three-year-old, and she picked the wrong nanny for him. She picked a woman who had no other life, who needed the emotional attachment too much and became too close to her child. It's a factor of hysteria."

▲

Mothers inherently have a strong influence over their children. You had just better decide what they're going to remember about you.

Pippa grew up in England. Her mother started working the minute she got out of school. At eighteen she was a saleslady in a shoe store, then became a commercial traveler, selling men's suits throughout the British Isles. In the forties, she got a job in the War Office in London, where she was a secretary for some officers and made it her business to know everything going on in Germany. Her husband had suffered several shrapnel wounds in the war and was put on a government pension that lasted the rest of his life. Though he took odd jobs under the table, he was the principal parent caring for Pippa and her brother, but she always saw him as someone in the background. It was her mother who had the strongest influence over her, the person she really wanted to emulate.

"Mum was working at the telephone exchange when I was little. I was very proud of her going to work. I thought she was very clever, but I missed her company during the day. Eventually, she was booted out of the telephone exchange for talking to her friends on the phone, and she took a job in London, which was an hour commute from our home in Reading.

"Since my mother was working, she shipped me off to an Irish boarding school when I was eleven. My parents came to see me once a week. My father would pick me up at vacations, and he'd always take me to the beautician to have a haircut and manicure before seeing my mother.

"I was a bit of a troublemaker in boarding school. I would go AWOL to the village or smoke in the stables or climb trees or something, and the nuns would call my mother to come to school. In a meeting, she'd say seriously, 'Oh, yes, she's very bad. We'll take her home and punish her. Would you excuse us a moment, please.' Then the nuns would leave the room, and my mother would laugh hysterically. My mother was really my friend.

"She understood children. She's very spirited and would do crazy things like break into dance suddenly or call out, 'Everyone to their secret hiding places!'

"We had a lot of fun. We were close, but going to boarding school I thought I lost a lot. My mother told her sister she regretted it, but never told me.

"My mother has a special gift. She's away and busy, but she has always held the whole family together. When she'd come home from work and see everybody down, she'd tell funny stories. She became chairwoman of the local Conservative Party and got us involved in politics. When anything happens to a family member, she takes charge.

"She was never a cuddler. But I know she loves me. She reminds me of a character from a Noël Coward play with all the quick wit and clever chatter. Still, she says, 'Wouldn't it be nice, Pippa, if you lived around the corner?'

"Growing up with her, I knew I could work when Paul was born."

▲

They say that a mother is allowed to make ten thousand mistakes. If you make just one big one, if you forget that your children are your priority, then all your mistakes count big-time.

Kara's mother is an executive in the financial world. They had live-in help when Kara and her brother were small.

"For a very high-powered person, she never brought work home. She came through the door as Mommy. She can compartmentalize her life. She made it clear that we were her priority. Our home was a loving, abundant place. No one was ever turned away. Friends were always welcome to stay for dinner and to sleep over. My mother came home every Friday afternoon with plans for us for the weekend. We could invite friends, and my mother would pay for everything. Do you think the mothers who didn't work were like this? No way. If I didn't know that I was the most important thing in the world to my mother, I would have resented her working very much."

Even though the mother has the greatest influence, sometimes the most important female in the house turns out to be the one Mother has hired to watch the children.

Vicki grew up in Michigan, where her mother was a psychologist.

"We lived in a normal middle-class community, but we were different because my mother worked, and we had Amanda living with us. I was very attached to her. She was everything my mother wasn't. She was cozy, warm, and around all the time. And because her *job* was cleaning, she didn't yell at us if we messed up the house. Every New Year's Eve, my parents went out, and Amanda stayed with my brothers and me. We'd go down to the basement for our own party, and she'd let us smoke.

"She left after many years, and we missed her a lot. My mother particularly missed her, and she sent her money. We stayed in touch for a while, but I don't know what happened to her. I wish she were around so I could tell her what she meant to me.

"I think I got so close to her because I was angry at my mother for being focused on her career. But now I understand it. You have to have a life away from your kids."

Okay, what about the other side of the coin, the flip side of this broken record of joy, joy, joy with wonderful caregivers? Ninety-nine percent of the stories you hear from mothers today are about nannies who have undisclosed criminal records or are gunning for them with behavior such as stealing the credit card numbers and charging everything on earth or loading up the vodka bottle with water or doing you-know-what in the middle of the living-room floor when Mom and the kiddies walk in.

Certainly, my mother did not have the good fortune always to hire a Sarah or a Tessie. There was Mary, who used to whack my brother and slide him across our polished foyer floor. We had Gussie, who was loaded in the afternoons, but it took until she was crying on the kitchen floor for us naive kids to call our mother at the office. And there was one weirdo couple we had living with us who got into a bloody brawl all through our house one night when my parents were out and sent my brother and me cuddling under the covers in terror. The couple ran out screaming and left us alone. When this woman was nuts enough to return to our house, my mother ordered her to pack and leave immediately. That's exactly what she did with the other misfits also.

My mother found that there's no such thing as a second chance when it comes to your children. If there's some inappropriate person caring for the children, then it's up to the parents to get rid of that person immediately. These caregivers are replaceable. It's a pain to find a new one, yes, but it's worse to keep a bad person in your house. You have to trust your children when they complain about somebody, believe that there's a problem, then investigate it. That's how our stories had a happy ending.

Today I am not left with a permanent, incurable nervous tic and a complete inability to leave my precious children in the care of any human who is not related to me. Instead, I have war stories, funny family memories that rank up there with the time fat cousin Madeline broke an antique chair in our living room. My brother and mother and I sit and laugh together about those old days. And my brother was the one who discovered he had hired the nanny with a hidden criminal record for his own children.

▲

Then, of course, there's Anna, who strikes a happy medium.

She grew up in a big city with a mother who was an important executive. Since her mother had waited until she was older to have children, she didn't want to give up her career, didn't want to move out to the suburbs to raise her children. She wanted to be close enough to stop home if a kid had chicken pox and to come home every evening at five for dinner, then go back to her office for a couple of hours when the phones had stopped ringing. Anna's dad was home early, too, because as a dentist he kept regular hours. They did have a competent nanny.

"We had Lila from the time I came home from the hospital. My mother's obstetrician suggested her. She became part of our family and stayed for fifteen years. She came at seven every morning and left after dinner. I can't say I had any great affection for her. I liked her well enough, but it was more fun to be around my mother.

"When my mother came home at night, she would play with the kids. My mother wasn't exhausted from taking care of us all day. It seemed like she *wanted* to see us. My friends had mothers who were at home, and they had no energy for their kids at night.

"She also made me realize that if you stop working when you have children, the world passes you by. You get out of touch with people. You don't know what's going on.

"It didn't matter that she didn't pick me up after school. I didn't miss anything. Today I feel very close to my mother. I know that she is the balance of things. Even now, with all us kids in our thirties, she still keeps the family together. It seems like what you always hear is the truth— your mother is the person to strive to be like."

Children who know what their mothers do all day at work are more inclined to tell their mothers what they do all day at school.

▲

O f the enormous number of mothers on this planet, you can count on one hand those who will ask, "What did you do at school today?" and not receive the reply, "I don't remember."

This is a particularly distressing fact for working mothers who are, for the most part, not picking their children up after school and having unscheduled chats with the teacher.

This answer is typical of all children. Once you give them the independence that you've carefully been meting out for years, they feel they're on their own, that you're butting in. Imagine sitting at the dining-room table every evening and being peppered with questions from *your* mother about how that ten o'clock meeting went and what the boss thought of your monthly numbers when you'd rather be lying on your bed reading comic books.

Nobody wants to answer a bunch of probing questions.

What's a working mother to do?

Suppose she acts like a caring, sharing relative rather than a U.S. attorney.

It might help if she realizes the benefits of disclosing her day to her children so that she and they can understand more about each other.

You know how the kindergarten teacher tells you to be specific with your child? Start out by asking about something nonthreatening, something safe, like lunch. Try it. Tell your kids what *you* had for lunch. Maybe you had *escargot,* a whole new thing. You'd be able to explain what it is, then the kids can start the conversation every evening by asking you whether today's lunch has been vichyssoise, cold mussels vinaigrette, or yogurt at your desk. You might even inspire them to expand their repertoire beyond the five basics: hot dogs, chicken nuggets, fries, chips, and gooey fruitlike things in a bag.

After a while, you'll see your way to discussing your *job* with your children. And they'll feel less than nailed to the wall when you ask them about math manipulatives.

My mother didn't have all the time in the world to talk to me as she wasn't around to see exactly what mood I was in when I came home from school. When I was little, she started something called Mother/Daughter Talks. We would lie on my bed in the dark and talk about people or things bothering us. I'd hear about crummy clients or dopey people in the office, and she'd hear about boys who pulled my hair, girls who stopped speaking to me, and teachers who were unbelievably unfair. As I got older, she could look at me and say, "Need a Mother/Daughter Talk?" We'd bop out to the car and go for a ride.

▲

Clearly, Mother can't do all the talking. You have to listen when the children tell you what's going on.

Candyce and her sister grew up over their mother's store. The fact that Marion's store happened to be a funeral parlor made for an unusual life.

Marion says, "This was my father's business. My first memory is at age three climbing up on the stool to watch my father do embalming. I got in the business right after college. My brother didn't want any part of it. It was too confining for him. But I couldn't see letting it out of the family.

"It became my whole life. My kids saw that and were used to it from infancy. Saturday night was the only night we could plan for because we had no viewings or funerals scheduled. I was a slave to the business."

Even though she was always in demand, Marion knew what her daughters were up to and laughs when she remembers how their little-kid antics put her busy work life in perspective.

"When they wanted to talk to me, they came downstairs and watched me doing makeup. They'd go to the viewings and say prayers. One night when one of my daughters was about three, she came downstairs without a stitch on to say a prayer at the kneeling rail. She looked at the woman who was laid out and said to me, 'She really looks nice. You did a beautiful job.'

"Sometimes they would put their dolls and cats in the display caskets. Once my father went up to show some caskets and found them filled with dolls. He was angry. I thought it was funny.

"The girls knew exactly what I expected of them. They couldn't run around the apartment and scream. There was always a funeral going on. I didn't have time to say no two or three times, and they knew it. If I needed somebody to answer phones, they would do it. They're very responsible.

They learned my basic belief: when you give your word, it's as good as something in writing.

"I gave them my word I would be around for them. They could always come to me. When everybody's mothers were too busy doing who-knows-what to take them roller skating, I would squeeze ten kids in a funeral limo.

"When it was Girl Scout cookie time, and the kids would tell me there was no place to store the cookies, I had them delivered right to the funeral home in an enormous tractor trailer.

"Even though the girls are grown, there's not a time they walk in that I don't get a kiss. I enjoy them as much now as ever."

Candyce, Marion's older daughter, is newly married and is a sales manager for a prestigious cosmetics company. Her mother had an enormous influence on the way she lives and does business.

"I like to deal with women," she says. "I think they try harder. When I was sick, I had a woman doctor, and she called me at home to check on me. It was the same kind of effort and compassion I saw my mother put out.

"I always saw my mother working. Whenever I wanted to talk to her, I never knew what I'd find her doing, but I didn't think about it. I knew other kids thought her job was weird, but I think my life was pretty good. I felt comfortable with her. She knew us so well.

"I'm her best friend. I felt guilty leaving her when I got

married. It was a big thing for me to call my mother-in-law 'Mom.' "

▲

Developing that kind of relationship over the years pays off in enormous dividends as the children get older. So rather than worrying about every single thing your kid is not telling you about school now, be concerned that you're building the trust that means your child can come to you when he's a grown-up. It's ever so much more important than knowing how many chapters he has to read in social studies.

Peter's mother was an elementary school teacher when he was small. She found it difficult to meet the needs of other people's children all day long and those of her own children when she came home at night. She left teaching and decided to go back into microbiology, which she had studied in college.

"She had to make an effort to do something new," says Peter, "and the work she had done twenty years before was not the best preparation. She took us kids right along with her in the struggle to overcome those barriers. We talked about it constantly.

"It was great to see my mom making an effort at *that age*. As children you see adults as fixed units. She changed my concept of what an adult is. My father always had the same job—he still has it—but my mother didn't want to be limited to a prescribed role.

"I inherited her nature to try new things. I work with computers. I take them apart. I saw her taking things apart at home when they were broken. I love camping because I saw that as an adult she decided she wanted to go backpacking with a tent. She found a colleague from work, and they hiked the Appalachian Trail.

"I am tremendously influenced by her. I have her vitality and excitement in looking at life. When we get together, we talk about ideas. People might interpret our conversations as arguments, but they're not. We challenge each other."

And Peter's mother, Sally, says, "It gets better as they get older when they talk to you and have a sense of logic and reasoning. It's a big step to be grown-ups together. Peter and I are very close, and he started calling me Sally. I said, 'We're two adults, but we still have the unique relationship of mother and son. You can call me Mother.'

"Besides, if I were just his friend, I wouldn't be included in so many events."

▲

Mutual respect and treating your kid as a thinking, growing human being contributes to a good relationship.

Alex's mother was a kindergarten teacher. When he and his sister were small, his mother would ask the children what sort of games she should play with the students. "She wanted us to be a part of what she was doing," he says, "just as much as she wanted input about teaching."

Susan grew up in Cambridge, where her father was a Harvard professor and her mother was a medical artist, rendering graphic depictions of operations and medical procedures, just the sort of stuff kids might giggle about unless their mother teaches them to respect what she does.

Susan says, "My mother had her studio at home, and while my sister and I were at school, she would be at her office at the hospital. Many days she would come home with Polaroids of an operation and talk to me about how she would draw it. I was very proud of her. I loved to watch her work.

"I was always impressed that my mother worked independently. It made me more self-reliant. My mother was busy when I got home from school. I was entirely responsible for how I spent my time. I had to find kids to play with and get there myself. My sister and I made up games.

We were good at entertaining ourselves. We weren't fussed over.

"As a result, I am more lenient about letting my kids troop around. I give them the time to enjoy their own company. I don't want them to be afraid of solitude. It's a gift my mother gave me.

"When I interviewed for my first job, I thought of my mother. The job was in book manufacturing and involved very detailed work I wasn't trained to do. I'd also have to work alone. I told my mother, 'If you can do it, I can do it.'

"The more we mothers can involve kids, the easier it's got to be for them. Let the kids see where you work.

"When my daughter challenged herself and entered a contest at school to design a schoolbook cover, she came to me for help. She knew I had the drawing board. I showed her how to do it, then left her alone.

"Having a teenager, I understand what my mother probably always knew. It doesn't all go in one ear and out the other. It comes back to you."

Working mothers are masters at including the kids and making everybody think it was a good idea.

▲

When you don't have children, you think microwave ovens are dangerous.

All those creepy rays beaming out when people should just stop off at the fishmonger every evening after work to select a couple of lovely salmon fillets to poach in a carefully made court bouillon.

You think station wagons are geeky. Backseats are superfluous. Point-and-shoot cameras are moronic. Video cameras are cumbersome. Vacations are meant for relaxation. Offices are meant for getting the job done.

People who talk all day about their kids are numbing. The kids themselves are sporadically tolerable.

But the worst thing you ever saw is people who dare to bring their kids along.

Oh, yes, those people who can't go out to dinner without the little ones, who couldn't step on a jetway without being sure a screaming thing is attached to their bodies, who become sightless and illiterate when signs say ADULTS ONLY, they're just too much.

Aren't they?

Heh, heh.

Waaaaah! Waaaaah!

The rules change.

The minute the baby arrives, you become one of *them*. You buy all that stuff you thought was ridiculous, you take pictures every forty seconds, have them developed immediately, then show them relentlessly to anyone who will listen. You nuke frozen, chemical-laden food and call it dinner. And if you thought you were busy before you had children, you are choked for space now.

Because now you have a *family*. A family that needs you as much as you need that job in order to keep them all in food, shelter, and clothing.

A working mother discovers that she has to find time

to be with her sweet little dearheart. She has to come up with those magic moments the magazines call "quality time." It's a silly notion because every time you're with your children is a quality time. Your child is experiencing you, finding out what you're about. Even if you're watching television together, you're still *together*. You don't have to be teaching your kid how to play chess or speak Japanese. You just have to give something of yourself.

Linda is an attorney in the Midwest and comes home exhausted every night from work. One evening, after she tucked her second-grader Nicholas into bed, his teacher phoned. She told Linda that Nicholas was falling behind in his reading group and that it seemed to her that Linda wasn't reading to Nicholas enough at night.

"It was true," says Linda. "I was so tired that I did everything I could just to get him fed, bathed, and into bed. I let him look at books by himself.

"I was crazy not to think about my own mother. She was in the magazine business and had to travel a lot. We didn't get as much time as I wanted together. When I was in fourth grade, I told her one night at dinner that I loved my class trip to hear the symphony. That night when she tucked me in, she asked me how I'd like it if she got tickets for the two of us to go to hear the orchestra every Thursday night.

"I was thrilled. It was nice for her because my father hated classical music and would never go with her. We kept it up until I went away to college. It was so successful that my mother got my sister interested in opera and took her every year when the Metropolitan Opera came to town. They studied the music and story. It was their big project together.

"I still can't promise to read with Nicholas every night. But I took him out of his Saturday morning tennis lesson. Now we go to a museum together.

"My mother never taught me how to make a pie crust. She taught me how to appreciate music. And that's made me have a very nice life."

▲

Sometimes including the children means bringing them to work. Working mothers find a way to tow them along so that everybody benefits.

When I was growing up, my mother had us come down to the office a lot. We tried not to get in the way. She'd usually set us up with markers and drawing pads in the art department of the advertising agency. When my children were born, and I would find myself occasionally without sitters, I would take them along.

The first time I showed up at a meeting with my son in a backpack, I acted as if nothing was unusual at all. No one wanted to say anything negative to me because they didn't want to appear insensitive to the working mother. When he started to fuss, I would stand up and sway back and forth. It killed my back, but I was able to get through the baby time just fine. I once took my daughter to a meeting when she was four months old, and she sat on a quilt next to the conference table playing with her toys. I remember looking over because she was so quiet, and saw that she had conked out all by herself.

Doing it in a pinch is one thing, stopping by after school is another, but regularly bringing your child to the office is not the world's greatest idea. I mean, how do you feel about women who can *never* find a babysitter? They don't have it together, and it probably reflects in their work.

One mother I talked to, who is a prominent attorney and just about ready to retire, said that she would be appalled if women brought their children to work on a regular basis. "I had my first child when I was still in college, my second when I was in law school. I always had to find somebody to take care of my children. It wasn't easy, it wasn't impossible. But women should be able to find child care," she told me, "and if they can't, then the corporation or government should help with it."

Ah, yes.

She believes in it so much she's working to pass a regulation in her city that all new office buildings be required to provide daycare.

▲

Mothers in certain professions are able to bring their children to work without much trouble.

Nadine's mother was the director of a community center near their home. She always worked long hours.

"When I was growing up I envied my friends," says Nadine. "Their mothers were home all day, and their houses were prettier and cleaner. We always had a big pile of laundry in the middle of the living room. Nobody cleaned house or cooked dinner. We ate out five out of seven nights.

"But we had something better. After school my brothers and sister and I would get dropped off at the community center. We got to take any classes we wanted. I was into drama, and when I was thirteen I was the only girl to take t'ai chi. I'm sure I wouldn't have been allowed to take so many classes if my mother hadn't been there. If my mother was home and had to drive us to classes after school, she probably would have complained the way other mothers did.

"I also liked that my mother was the boss. I felt proud of her. And I was a big shot."

Judy grew up in Philadelphia, where her mother was a curator of decorative arts at the Philadelphia Museum of Art. Her mother worked every weekend giving gallery talks, and because she and her husband were separated, and there was no one to look after her five children, she took them along.

"We were at the museum all weekend," recalls Judy. "We saw movies, Punch and Judy shows, took art classes. I picked my favorite paintings and would hang out in front of them.

"It made me learn a lot about my mother, too. One Sunday in 1941, she was scheduled to give a lecture on the Japanese artist Hiroshige. When she presented the lecture, the audience started to boo. I was six years old, and I began to cry. I didn't understand what was going on."

It was December 7: what she didn't understand was that the Japanese had just bombed Pearl Harbor that morning. "So they weren't booing Mother. She became a real heroine to me. She was so poised. I was impressed she could take it."

Don's mother was national president of the League of Women Voters and had to travel weekly. She was always going to Washington from their home in Louisville, and when Don had vacation time, she took him along.

"If it had bothered me that my mother traveled so much, I'd have been one unhappy kid," he says. "I met people my mother was working with, and I got to go to some debates. These were very interesting to me. But, of course, what I really remember was playing chess with the 'sharks' in Dupont Circle near our hotel in Washington. And winning!"

Pam grew up in New York, where her mother was an actress. "She would go on the road for weeks at a time," says Pam. "Once, when I was five, she had my father and me fly out to California to be with her. Disneyland had just opened, and we went for a visit.

"Sometimes I came to watch her shows in New York. She did industrial shows, and she introduced the Mustang to the world. It was a big extravaganza in New York. I remember seeing her flying through the air. She came whizzing down to a platform where she sang about the joys of the Mustang. I was pretty impressed."

▲

Many times one of the greatest advantages of growing up with a working mother is the exposure to sophistication at an early age.

Sandy's mother was an editor in publishing and brought interesting people around. "I was always being exposed to people who were not what you get in the playground set," Sandy remembers. "My mother knew an artist, and when I was little and fascinated with animals, I made her draw squirrels for four hours. My mother took me to lunch with people who spoke foreign languages, and I was awed. One of her friends had the most amazing style. She had no husband or children, and she lived in an exquisite apartment that was like a jewel box. I really learned what taste is.

"Another of my mother's associates had a daughter my age, so when she and my mother had to have a business lunch, the daughters would get to go along during school vacations. We ordered things like artichokes when we were just ten.

"I liked these lunches and meetings. I felt I belonged there. The business people liked me, and I knew it. They were warm and loving."

It's another way to learn who your mother is. She's not just the one who's screaming at you to pick up your toys or turn out your light at night or eat a vegetable once every six months. She's also this adult who does adult things.

Leslie wasn't all that sure what her stockbroker mother did for a living.

"She was really in charge at home. I had a very clear idea of what being a together, confident woman was about," says Leslie. "My mother was a single parent. She came from a lower-class farming family that always worked. The notion of a genteel housewife doesn't exist in my family."

Still, her day-to-day existence at the office was a mystery.

"When I was in high school, my mother thought it was time for me to understand what she did. She took me on one of those trips to the islands that the brokers win when they do well. There were no other women brokers on this trip. I was impressed that she could keep up with the men.

"I liked us having a vacation together. She worked so hard we never went away, and all of her money was for college.

"On this trip she won a jacket. Of course, she was the only woman with one. One night at dinner we sat with some Texans. The husbands were at the bar, the wives talking at the table. My mother said, 'None of these women will talk to me if they think I'm the broker. Let's just be a couple of ladies.'

"One of these Texan wives looked over at my mother wearing the jacket and said, 'I didn't know you could have a matching jacket like your husband's.'

"My mother didn't say, 'No, I'm the broker.' Instead, she said, 'I just took the patch off Bob's jacket and put it on mine.'

"Should I have cried because there was no Bob or because I was so proud of her? It taught me a lot."

▲

Working mothers also have to remember that they're raising children. Special events with them have to be those that are fun for children.

Amy's mother never let the silly child in her grow up. So even though she would always tell Amy, "Have respect for what each passing year gives you in insight," she would still do spur-of-the-moment things with her.

"In high school on a beautiful spring day, my mother woke me up and said, 'Let's go to Atlantic City. No school for you. No work for me.' The greatest. We didn't tell anybody. We drove down for the day. We lay on the beach in our clothes and got sunburned. We wondered what people were saying about us and whether we were reported as missing persons. We ate seafood, walked on the boardwalk, ate saltwater taffy.

"Every summer we went up to Nantucket. My mother would get up before dawn, pack up food, a big old skillet, newspaper, and matches, wake me quietly, and we'd bike to the beach. We collected wood, built a fire, and cooked breakfast. We didn't talk much. Then we'd bike back to the house and go to sleep. She could have done it by herself, but I loved that she chose me."

Elena is a chef, a wonderful Italian chef. She talks about recipes she invents, how to find the best butcher, what to ask for, which olive oil to use, which wine is best with veal. How does she know all this? From her mother, who had a restaurant in Italy.

"When I create a new dish, I visualize my mother standing in the restaurant kitchen. Without moving, she could reach everything, the refrigerator, spices, knives, olive oil, stove. She was right in the middle. I sat on a stool watching, but I said I would never cook. I thought my mother worked too hard.

"My mother never said anything, just encouraged me to sit in the kitchen with her so we could talk. After a few years, I would help her a bit. Chopping or something. I started to like it. And, of course, I had a natural talent. So subtle, wasn't she?

"We spend so much of our lives looking for something or someone to tell us what we should do. We don't stop to look inside, see where our strength comes from."

**A working mother will give up
a limb for her children.
It's just that she has to arrange
for time off first.**

▲

an't you just see yourself having one of these superhuman adrenaline rushes and lifting a car off your child if it should come to that?

You'd run into a flaming building to rescue your darling bunnyface and then leap out a third-story window, right?

Don't you try to prevent your precious little ones from listening to the news, overhearing fights and unrepeatable comments about dreadful relatives to keep them safe and innocent as long as possible?

Natch.

But anybody can do all that.

It takes a working mother to risk losing her job, her livelihood, all her money, her spouse, and her dignity so she can do those intrinsic mother things for her children.

Betty is a college professor in Pittsburgh, and her grown, yes, grown, son who lives in New York City called one evening to say that he had a terrible cold and sore throat. Betty immediately jumped into her car, drove to the drugstore, picked up a bevy of cold remedies and throat lozenges one couldn't possibly find in New York, then rushed them over to the Federal Express office before the last shipment of the day so that her *grown* son wouldn't have to get out of bed the next morning to get his own darn medicine. "Fortunately," says Betty, "I know it never stops, and I can laugh about it."

When my son was three, he held in high regard a friend of ours who makes violins. My son announced that he wanted to play the violin, and I replied that he could take lessons when he was four. Fully expecting him to be disinterested, I was held to my word when he reminded me at age four that he could now take lessons. Okay, okay. You can give a little kid violin lessons, but did you know the *mother* has to play along? I had about as much time for this as I had to make cupcakes. Plus I had no musical talent.

Well, I learned to play, and now that my son has given it up, of course, I am still taking violin lessons. I am still scratchy, squeaky, and my teacher Gustav keeps telling me to listen to the way *he* plays so that I can make the violin "sing." But I enjoy it.

Who am I kidding? I keep doing it because I think that if my son hears *me* practicing, he'll take it up again.

The motivation to do this has everything to do with being a mother, nothing to do with being a working mother bursting with guilt.

I remember my own mother's thinking that I had to take music lessons. I chose piano. She chose the meanest teacher on earth. Even worse, my mother could not take me to piano lessons at normal after-school hours. So she talked the teacher into giving me lessons at seven-thirty on Tuesday mornings. She even convinced one of her friends that *her* daughter should go out that hour, too, so that I shouldn't have to be tortured alone. My mother went through all this, and yes, I did quit.

▲

There are a lot of mothers who are practically killing themselves for their children. And it's not just for music lessons. It's not just for a second VCR to anesthetize them or a Beemer for some nanny to cart them around in.

It's for survival. Those of us who are lucky can look at the world as being filled with choices. We agonize over them, pay thousands of dollars to lie on a couch and agonize to somebody else. That's our life. That's our gift. Many mothers live in a world of do or die.

"When I got out of college, women worked because they were swept up in the women's movement and wanted to have some power," says Carol. "Suddenly, women weren't graduating and getting married. Our educations were for our careers.

"Now that we have children, many of us *have* to work. As I get to know more of the mothers dropping off their children at my son's nursery school, I find that they're the keepers of today's deep, dark secret: their husbands are out of work, and the wives are bringing home all the money there is."

▲

This is hardly the first time in history that women have had to contribute to the family income. There have always been times when Mother's income wasn't to make ends meet but to get things started in the first place. And, honest, it doesn't scar the kids for life. In fact, it can make them pretty savvy.

Margot's mother taught before her children were born. She took time off to be with them when they were small, then went back to work when the youngest went to first grade. Even though, as Margot says, "My mother's idea of being productive was more than making beds and dinner," she soon learned she'd have to produce an income for her family. Margot's father lost his high-paying powerful job, and suddenly stopped commuting, working, and thinking positively. He took various jobs through the years, but none ever paid as well, and Margot's mother delicately assumed the role of ringmaster.

"When my mother went back to work," says Margot, "my father was still in his big job and wasn't real happy she was working. He told her, 'You're going to have to make it work. I still expect dinner on the table when I come home.' Well, that was the fifties. She did make it work. Then he lost his job, and things changed. We all had to make it work. I remember lists and lists. We all had jobs and responsibilities.

"Organization I remember clearly. If I wanted to do something different after school, she'd say, 'You may do that, but I will be at the library at four to pick you up.' If I screwed up, I'd be in trouble. There was the notion that if I made it harder for her, I made it harder for everybody. She was furious with me when I got sick. I have a vivid memory of having a sore throat. She got mad because it meant that somebody had to stay home. I'd wonder, 'Where do my allegiances lie?'

"How could I let her down? She was the Brownie leader, too, and she made the best birthday parties with special themes and always let us invite a dozen friends.

"Though my mother loved to work, she thinks today that her working so hard was difficult for the children. 'It wouldn't have been like that if I had been at home,' she says, 'but it didn't happen that way.'

"She shouldn't ever, ever feel guilty," says Margot. "To this day, I feel this experience is something that influenced me. I have trouble with a mother who sets herself up as a great provider and gives her children no responsibility."

Phoebe was handed a load of responsibilities when she was a teenager. Her parents divorced, and she and her sisters stayed with their father, who got the house. "My father's business was bankrupt, so my mother supported us because she was a well-paid psychologist.

"My mother was absent but not apart. She felt so

guilty for leaving. She'd call me with ballet tickets, ask me whether she could come to speak at Career Day at school. I'd come home and find she had left one hundred fifty dollars' worth of food in the refrigerator. And to make sure we'd eat it, she paid me twenty-five dollars a week to cook. She was never forced to do any of this by the courts. Judges didn't seem to think about a woman's income in those days. I got financial aid when I went to college because the school never thought to look at my mother's finances. I was the beneficiary of a narrow-minded establishment.

"My mother taught me to be independent even before she left. She expected me to do things around the house and trained me to do it. She believed we should be able to get anywhere on our own. She always gave me the freedom to do whatever I wanted. You need this in your early teen years. I couldn't believe in high school that mothers were still making their kids' lunches."

When John was in fourth grade, he developed meningitis. His mother quit working in a big university science lab to care for him for the several months he would have to be home.

"It was so boring lying in bed all day. My mother and I read magazines together," says John. "We saw a story in *National Geographic* about a nineteen-year-old boy who sailed alone around the world. My mother thought that the two of us should plan a trip around the world. So we took a month and a half to plan and sail an imaginary voyage. We decided the kind of boat we would need, the provisions and clothes that were appropriate. It was just like that integrated curriculum that's so popular now in school. You don't realize you're really learning something.

"This was the first time I realized my mother was so interesting and adventuresome. That intense time together gave us the basis for a close relationship that has lasted through the years."

▲

Then there are those mothers who truly go to the ends of the earth for their children.

Miriam is an attorney who admits she always led "a crazy, frenetic life. I always had energy to do what I wanted to do, and I wanted to do all of it.

"When my son Robert was away at college, he took his junior year abroad. I came home one day to find a letter from him. He sounded very sad, unlike himself, so I quickly called him and said, 'Will you clear your schedule and meet me in London for four days?' He agreed. I got on the phone and rented an apartment. I needed to be able to bake brownies and cook all the American food I knew he missed. I packed a suitcase with clothes for me and another with food for him.

"Never mind that I was in the middle of trying a case. The next morning I went to the judge and said, 'I have a commitment to meet my son. I must leave today at four

o'clock, and I will try the case again Thursday morning.'
The judge gave me a recess. I presented it as if he had no
choice.

"Robert and I spent four days running around. We
went to the theater, to the Royal Academy, even to the
London Zoo. One afternoon we stopped for tea, and I was
reading the paper. 'Look, Robert,' I said, 'Curtis Mayfield
is in town, and I think we can catch him after the symphony tonight.'

"My twenty-year-old son closed his eyes. 'Mom, I
don't think I can do so many things at once.'

"I took a pencil and paper out of my purse. 'Make a
note of it. Your mother was ready to take you to Curtis
Mayfield, and you turned her down.'

"There was no question I would have done anything
for him. And I did cure his homesickness."

▲

Working mothers have to learn that time off doesn't
necessarily mean time alone. It can be a great time to
get away with your child, get to know her better, share
some of your values, your experiences, your most precious
thoughts.

When each child in Hannah's family turned twelve,
their working mother took them on their own private
mother/kid trip to New York for a weekend.

"Mother had us send for information about New York so that we could plan just what we wanted to do. The only limitations we had were budgetary. I remember blowing my entire budget on a helicopter ride around the Statue of Liberty so we spent a lot of our weekend walking around New York. But this was a coming-of-age event that we looked forward to for years. It was a time to be alone with her. I would do the same thing with my children."

Margaret told me the story of her mother, a story of sacrifice that grabs you right in your motherly heart. Margaret was one of five children, and grew up in the thirties and forties. In the mid-forties, Margaret's mother left her alcoholic husband and took her children to live in the three-room apartment she could afford. Still, she had to work two jobs. Her night job was editing the company newspaper for the Pennsylvania Rail Road from ten until seven-thirty in the morning. After work she'd come home to find the kids waiting at the curb for her trolley to pull up. She'd get them all off to school, get some sleep, and be at her day job from ten in the morning until four in the afternoon, when they'd all be waiting for her again at the curb. They would get her to bed and do their homework in silence to let her sleep.

"Mother never had a day off both jobs at the same time," says Margaret. "My grandmother wanted to put us in foster homes, but my mother said no, that she could do it. She'd tell us the way we lived was temporary. To try to prove it to herself, she arranged for us to go to the best schools. Some of us were in private school, some in special public schools. I don't know how she managed this.

"My mother always did a big thing for Christmas. It was something she couldn't possibly have afforded. But every Christmas Eve our rich Uncle Edward and Aunt Ruth would appear with lots of gifts for us. They weren't our real relatives, but they acted like it. Now I suspect they must have helped pay for us to go to college and send my brother to medical school.

"I never knew how they met my mother. But when I was in my forties, and Aunt Ruth had already died, I invited Uncle Edward to dinner. When we were having drinks, I asked him how they had come to be our fairy godparents.

"He sipped his drink and leaned forward in his chair. 'In 1938,' he told me, 'Ruth and I moved to town. We had never had any children nor had any family here, and we were lonely.

"'One day I read a classified ad in the paper asking for an older couple who wanted to make Christmas for five children. Aunt Ruth and I answered the ad. The woman who placed it was your mother.'

"I was stunned. Is there any wonder my mother is my hero?"

**The bad news is your mother's not
there when you get home
from school. The good news is
your mother's not there when you
get home from school.**

▲

on't tell the airlines this. If they ever thought
they were doing something for working moth-
ers, they would turn it into some kind of patronizing commercial that would drive all of us insane.

The fact is they have a little gimmick for working
mothers.

When you book a flight, you can ask the on-time percentage of that flight. Maybe the two o'clock is 70 percent on time, and the three o'clock is 90 percent on time. Of course, you'd choose the three o'clock. Because when *you* jump off the plane, you have to sprint to baggage claim, leap into your vehicle, and rocket home to be with the kids. Anything for a few extra minutes.

So what if you're missing that five o'clock urgent meeting? You invent some critical reason, other than your children, to get out of it.

When the kids are little, they'll be appreciative of your brilliance and planning. They'd love to hear a book, do a puzzle, squish Play-Doh. By the time they're six or so, it won't make a whole bunch of difference. Because after school, they'd rather be playing with their friends, beating up their siblings, or spacing out in front of the television.

In other words, *they don't want you around!*

Guilt still bubbling up inside?

Why bother?

As Anthony says, "My mother went to work as an executive secretary when the last of us kids went to kindergarten. She didn't hire anyone to take care of us. My brother, who was three years older, was home. I don't remember if she came to school plays or anything. Who can remember anything from when they were little? I know she was involved. So what if she wasn't home every day? It made me independent very early."

In his case, the independence paid off. He describes

himself as "a bit of a rascal" and starts his own computer software businesses with great regularity.

There's something to this business of not being home.

Just gaze into your past and apply it to your future. Was your mother home after school? Did she try to give you healthy snacks? Or impossibly fattening ones? Did she quiz you half to death? Did she want to take you shopping? Ask you to do errands?

My little darling son is happy to see me that first minute or two after he gets home, but then he's off on his own. If in my attempt at togetherness I save an errand to do with him that does not involve going to the toy store or the dinosaur museum, he'll sit in the car and tell me how bored he is.

And you know what happens by the time your children are teenagers. They *really* don't want you at home.

According to Wendy, "Kids would come to my house after school because my mother wasn't home. My best friend and I could try smoking and blow the smoke out the window. We could read dirty books and laugh. Sometimes we practiced backing the car out of the garage. This is normal stuff, but it was easier to do at my house. Mothers know what you're doing every second."

▲

A lot of teenagers have less than civil relationships with their mothers. Many of these mothers are thankful they have careers, since many know they would turn into screamers if they stayed home.

Rona knows this is what would have happened with her mother. "I know she felt guilty for not being around, but I never complained. She always had to defend herself. When she would come home very late at night, she'd wake me up to ask me how I was doing. It was exasperating. I'd say, 'Mom, do you have to wake me up now?'

"My favorite thing when I was a teenager was coming home to an empty house. I could eat what I wanted, leave my stuff all over the place and not have my mother yell at me to pick it up. When she came home at night we argued a lot."

As one mother said, "I am not a homebody. I have to have something that challenges me. Housework and cooking challenge me but in a way that makes me angry and frustrated. I don't believe mothers are put on this earth to wait on children hand and foot. So I gave my children chores and paid them minimum wage. If they did extra chores, they got more money. They tried. I got a tolerance for a certain level of dust. But if I had been home all day,

I would have gone crazy screaming at them and felt put upon that I had to do everything."

▲

Then there are some mothers who feel guilty for not being around and, in turn, overlove their children.

Lauren's mother was a conductor and worked very long hours. In public she was aggressive and outgoing, yet shy and closed about her private life. With her own kids, says Lauren, "she was a mushball. It was always, 'I want to take care of you. Let me do everything for you.'

"Sometimes it was embarrassing how much she loved me. I thought, 'Thank God she works. She's smothering enough as it is.' I saw her the right amount of time each day."

▲

Certain children have busy lives and don't seem to notice one way or the other whether their mothers are home, though they still know who runs the show.

"By the time I was in high school," says Nancy, "I had sports after school. I would get home at six, eat dinner, then study. On the days I didn't have sports, I would go to a friend's house to talk. My mother certainly wasn't removed or distant. In fact, she had very clear rules. Because we lived in the middle of the city, she was obsessed with safety and was very stern with us. She let us know that we shouldn't make any stupid mistakes.

"I was very proud of my mother and close to her. I could talk to her about anything. I didn't need her around every minute. I wasn't even there."

Elizabeth's family lived in New York. Her mother worked long hours as a stockbroker. But she kept her children busy with certain after-school jobs so that the family could be together when she got home. The independence gave Elizabeth real confidence.

"When I got to fifth grade I could handle things myself," says Elizabeth. "In the morning my mother would leave a note regarding the food she wanted me to make for dinner. I had a little budget to do shopping and did it myself. The people in the little stores on Second Avenue would ask, 'Where's your mommy?' I felt so grown up. My brother had laundry duty and had to figure how many loads he could do with the allocated number of quarters. My brother and I also did the housework and would fight about who had to do which job. I was older and tried to discipline him, but my mother made it clear I was not the mother, that she was the ultimate arbitrator. Another rule was to get our homework done before she came home so we could talk to her. She really taught me the importance of being organized. And I think I learned it better because she wasn't around."

Chuck knows he was a lot better off having a working mother who wasn't on top of him every second. His mother has two masters degrees and was one of the first African American women to graduate from New York University Law School. She started out working as a dancer at the Cotton Club in Harlem and then used her shrewd business mind to buy houses in Harlem and become a real estate broker. As tough as she was in business, that's how hard she was on him.

"My mother believed in work. Her mind was always on what she was doing. She'd come home at night, and we'd sit and talk about the deals she'd done that day or what she had learned in school. I thought it was great.

"Her ideas about me were different from what I thought I should do. When I was a teenager, she told me that a male was not supposed to be a sissy, that I had to learn to take care of myself. So I caddied, worked in restaurants. She was very structured as far as my schooling went. She thought sciences or law were the way to go. I'm more creative, interested in spirituality. She even put a damper on athletics. I ran the mile when most African Americans were running the dash. She wanted me to stay away from sports. But today I'm a marathon runner.

"If she had been home all the time, we would have driven each other crazy. My family left Harlem for St. Albans in Queens along with people like Jackie Robinson, Count Basie, and Roy Campanella. I hated it. I didn't like middle-class people. In the civil rights revolution, I became very active. My mother was not. She did believe in the struggle, but she had individual goals. I had group goals.

"We argued and argued. We finally came to an agreement. I said, 'You live your life, I'll live mine. We are two strong-willed people. And no matter what, we must always love each other.' Today she's in her eighties. We still give each other the space to love and respect one another."

▲

There are some children of working mothers who object very loudly to their mothers *not* being home.

Mildred was the first woman professor at the University of Pennsylvania. She broke the barrier in the university with her appointment at the medical school. Her career is a modern history of discrimination against women. In the 1920s women were able to study chemistry in college only because "they thought we would teach," she says.

The chairman of the chemistry department approached her when she wanted to get an advanced degree. "If you persist in this misguided path," he told her, "you will be coming to me in a year for different advice. You will have met a fifty-five-year-old widower with five children and ask me whether you should marry him."

"Who wants five children?" she answered.

But her family came first. She married a scientist ("You have to marry the right man if you're going to have a career and family"), had three children ("I spent all my money on child care and housekeepers"), and compartmentalized her life ("I never talked about the children at work"). She kept herself off the fast track so that she would be able to be home by six o'clock every evening to be with her three children. She and her professor husband took unpaid leaves every summer to go away *en famille*. She had a housekeeper who stayed for twenty years while the children were growing up. She tried to make life as stable as possible for her children.

But one objected, because Mother had to work on Saturdays.

"My oldest daughter wanted me at every PTA meeting, which I was, but her complaining didn't stop," says Mildred. "In those days you went to college six days a week. She hated that I worked on Saturdays, so one Saturday when she was eight, I stayed home. All day long she ran in and out of the house with her friends. I never saw her. At dinner I said, 'You complain about my not being here but you were nowhere to be seen all day long, and I was here to be with you.'

"'I don't want to be with you,' she answered. 'I just want you here.'

"My son didn't care if I was home. My youngest daughter said, 'What would you do if you stayed home all day? Play bridge? You'd be boring!'

"When my oldest daughter got to college she called to tell me she had the most marvelous idea for a term paper.

It was going to be on the children of working mothers versus the children of nonworking mothers. She was going to prove that a working mother wreaked havoc on her children. She called with great disappointment after she had done her research. 'I can't prove my theory,' she said. 'There's no evidence.'

"'I'm a scientist. I could have told you that,' I answered.

"My children all went on to get Ph.D.s. My daughters are psychotherapists, my son is a cell biologist who works in a lab with his wife. They all have children, and they're quite content."

▲

But did you hear the one about the mother who wasn't home every afternoon, and her kid was the most screwed up one in the school?

Alice says, "I was the wildest of the four kids. In high school people hung out at my house because my mother wasn't there. I brought the worst kids home. It also gave me room for cutting school, and my mother was never home to get calls from the truant officer. I was the rebel.

"My brothers and sister were responsible and normal. They didn't do drugs, were on the chess team and tennis team, did well in school, and went to plays. I didn't want to be like them. I didn't like their middle-class values.

"Right before I finished high school, I discovered I really liked writing. I loved words. I was interested in the world around me, and I was always writing about it. I won an award for aspiring journalists. I quit doing drugs. I realized I had some talent. It wasn't like my mother's, my brothers' or sister's. It was mine. Fortunately, I graduated from high school, and my parents put me into college.

"When I went away to college and would tell people what my mother did, they said I was lucky. They wished their mothers did something. I realized that I had not been brought up to be only a housewife.

"I grew up thinking women run the household, that women can do anything they want to. A woman could be president of anything. She could be successful, she could be something.

"Now I'm a journalist, and my mother is my biggest fan. She shows every article I write to everyone she works with."

▲

See, you can't blame everything on the mother, but sometimes you can place a lot of it on her. Especially if she *is* working and *is* home but neglects to find out how her children are doing. Yes, a mother can be absent after school, but she can't be twice removed.

Tom's mother was a psychotherapist who had an office at home, but she wasn't exactly there. What was there were a secretary, a nursemaid, a cook, a laundress, a housekeeper, and a houseman. When Tom got involved with drugs, he says, "She let me know implicitly that she wasn't crazy about the idea but that she trusted my judgment and sense of responsibility." Apparently, that sense of his was not overdeveloped, because his mother got a call from one of his teachers, who said "I hadn't been at school for the last week or so. She answered, 'I haven't seen him either, so if he comes to school, ask him to call home.' " Charming.

Fortunately, Tom is considerably more involved with his own three children. He's a writer, has flexible hours, and, he says, "I can't think of anything I'd rather be doing."

And maybe there's something working mothers never think about because we're so worried about what we're doing wrong. There might be something we're doing right.

As Gina looks back on it from a grown-up perspective, she says, "I always knew where my mother was if I had to find her after school. She was at her office. I never thought that maybe she was out on the tennis court or something. It gave me the sense that I was always supported by her."

Working mothers do not have to ask Daddy for money. Neither do their children.

▲

n those old thirties movies that are too horrible to be at revival houses but too good to be missed, you often find an innocent, apple-cheeked young person who gets into trouble and tries to get out of it alone. After attempting several solutions and failing, the kid breaks down in a cathartic scene in the kitchen with Mom and tells her that the world as we know it will end unless that kid gets $17.52 from God-knows-where to repair the broken window or to buy new costumes for the class play or to contribute to the best friend's iron-lung fund.

Mom, of course, puts the whole thing into perspective and climbs up on a ladder to the top cabinet where she pulls out a hidden jar stuffed with dollar bills.

The kid's eyes widen. Mom explains, "This is my butter and egg money. I always put some aside from the profits in my business. And it's for emergencies like this. It's our little secret."

Kid, eternally grateful, goes off to fight another battle. Mom, ever the protector of her young, looks heavenward to express thanks that she has an income.

It hasn't changed, folks.

Working mothers are still able to make terrific magic with their money.

In economic times that more frequently than not call for two family incomes to let one family live up to basic standards, the income of the working mother is a necessity. But earning her own money lets Mother be the guardian and patron she wants to be. Sometimes a few bucks mixed in with Mom's kisses, hugs, and good wishes can give kids a lot of confidence and make them understand that Mom really does trust them after all.

If the money is earned by the mother and the children ask her for something directly, the working mother can feel that the decision was a *she,* not a *we* that she has to agree upon with her male counterpart. It makes her feel that her contribution to the family is powerful.

When Barbara was growing up in the thirties and forties, her mother was an elementary school teacher. Her mother made important additions to the everyday life of the family and never kept it a secret.

"I learned," says Barbara, "that if you work you have money to make more things possible. My mother was very proud of having an income. She had much more say and influence over decisions because she was paying her share. The first time we bought a car, my mother said, 'My money made this possible.' If we wanted to take a vacation, and my parents weren't agreeing about where to go, she'd say, 'My money will pay for it.' I have a feeling my father wanted to save all his money, that he didn't want to splurge. She didn't live like that at all.

"When my children were very young, I didn't work. I thought, 'I have this good education. I am not stupid. Why am I reading recipes?' I started volunteer work, but a volunteer is not respected. Our society puts a value on how much you're making.

"I went to work as a mathematician. Immediately, I opened my own checking account. I had *my* money so that I could do things for the children. I didn't spoil them. They all worked toward college. I gave them a certain amount of money each semester, and they had to live with it and allocate it themselves. I think it's demeaning to have to ask for money.

"Now that they're grown, I still send them money when they're not expecting it. It's a little icing on life. If I see there's a good play in New York, I'll send my oldest daughter a check for two tickets and tell her to take somebody.

"She and I share a checking account. I probably put most of the money into it. I tell her not to bother reimbursing me. Now that I have money, I'm very lax about it.

"My son came to us when he wanted to buy a house and asked for money. I told him it was a loan. I don't believe parents should buy houses for their children. My husband and I gave him money separately. My husband worked out an elaborate payback system. I immediately forgot about it. Whatever my son sent me was fine.

"When one of my daughters got married, she was visiting, and I thought she and her husband would like to have a nice dinner, so I gave her a check and told her to go to a good restaurant.

"But once when she was packing up to leave, I gave her money, and she said, 'That's okay, Mom, Daddy gave me some. Don't bother.' I never knew about it, never discussed it with him, and never told him I send the children money."

Delia grew up in Chicago with a very traditional father and a very nontraditional mother whose income changed their lives.

"My father never wanted my mother to work. He had a narrow concept of how people were supposed to live. He wanted us to live in a cute little bungalow. He wanted a Donna Reed housewife who wore dresses all the time. Hardly what he got.

"She was a Joan Crawford suit type. She liked the idea of being able to take care of herself. By the time they were married, my mother was already established in her career.

"Her money significantly contributed to my brother's and my development. She sent us away to a special, expensive music camp every summer. We knew she paid for vacations. And every time we wanted to go to the symphony, she made sure we had the best seats. The benefits were tremendous."

▲

Lest you think all these mothers ran out and bought cars for their children, think again. Having this extra income doesn't call for a working mother to spoil her children rotten. Rather, she tends to give them a respect for money and an understanding of what it is used for and, of course, the truth that it does not grow on trees.

When Ginny and her sisters became teenagers, their working mother decided it was time to teach them about money. So she gave them clothing allowances.

"We felt free to choose what we wanted," says Ginny. "She wanted us to learn how to spend money and how to allocate it. So we got a lump sum at the beginning of each semester. I was the one who looked for bargains so I could have more for my money. One sister liked quality, so she always had fewer clothes, but she probably still has some of them in her closet. My other sister didn't buy much. She was good at saving her money. We got a good sense of how much clothes cost."

Erin's mother started her own business when Erin and her sister were little. She worked hard, eventually made more money than her husband, but put most of her income into a pooled fund so that nobody really knew whose money was paying for what.

As Erin says, "I never went without, but I really don't think I was spoiled. My allowance was never huge. It started at five cents a week and went up to three or five dollars when I was older. But I was expected to take out the trash and do chores around the house in order to get it! I worked in high school as a sales clerk in a pharmacy and then for my mother and earned enough money to buy my own car. I had to pay for gas, too. My mother taught me that money is one measure of success, but she was never obsessed by it."

Natalie's mother taught her that money "was there to spend if necessary. I saw that money saved her time. She could buy the more expensive item rather than shopping around for the bargain. And a working mother certainly doesn't have time."

▲

Most of the working mothers I met did not grow up with the money their children did. They struggled. Their money is what gave them their independence. This was not lost on their grown children.

Mara's mother grew up in South America in a working-class family. "She always wanted to be somebody," says Mara. "She wanted to go to the United States. Her mother had tried to leave but couldn't do it financially. My mother wanted to know she could take care of herself. She did odd jobs to pay for her schoolbooks and her education. She is a proud woman and believes no one will rescue you. You have to rely on yourself.

"I didn't grow up wealthy. She made more and more money as the years went on. I envied her because she had to struggle for what she wanted. I always thought that people who are deprived are more focused. She made me work in high school so that I could help with my college tuition payments. I had a real sense of accomplishment and of myself."

Paula is a retired high school English teacher with four children. She lived in the upper-middle-class community in which she taught. Most of the mothers did not work. It just wasn't done. But Paula is very smart, very intellectual, and there was no doubt she would teach.

"At first, I tried to tell myself I wasn't doing it for the money. But it got to be a lot of money, and it began to matter. There were years I would have quit if it didn't mean money. I started to invest my money in old houses. I rehabbed them and sold them at a great profit. Since I did very well, I was able to be very generous with my children. Now they all have excellent jobs. Still, they need help from me sometimes, and they pay back promptly.

"In a sense, I'm sorry they grew up in my school district. Everybody there really had more money than they needed, and my children didn't get a sense of struggling. But only one is spoiled. My son buys every new thing that comes out. It seems like such a self-indulgent waste. But I'm waiting for him to have children. He hasn't had to make those parental sacrifices yet."

▲

Truly, though, it's the nature of working, of producing an income, of deciding how to spend it, of having responsibility for a corporate bottom line that makes a *working* mother's money and attitudes different.

It makes her advice seem a lot more like Dad's used to be. You know, important.

When Audrey's mother was thinking about leaving the museum job she loved for one that paid more money, the kids all said, "Oh, Mom, stay in the job you love. So what if you don't have money. We'll take care of you when you retire."

Mom said sagely, "I must take care of myself. You'll want to take care of me, but you won't be able to. You'll have your own families. I have to take the new job. I need the benefits. I need medical coverage and a retirement plan."

"It was shocking to us," says Audrey. "But she was right. When I look for jobs, I ask about the benefits package. When my daughter took her most recent job, I asked how much she was making a week. It didn't seem to me she was earning enough. She told me she was earning as much as her babysitter. But she explained she had to keep the job because the benefits were tremendous—even better than her husband's. She put him on her medical plan. I guess I taught her something."

The advice that used to be Dad's domain seeps through in many ways.

Cara was a nurse and raised a few daughters. She noticed that one did not have the slightest idea about money.

She went to her daughter and said, "You have developed a proclivity for the good life, and the job you have chosen for yourself will not sustain it. There are three ways to get money. Number one: earn it. Number two: inherit it. And don't count on that. I don't have it, and I don't believe in it. Number three: marry it. I think you should consider that option."

And she did.

It used to be that Dad would sit down with his son, probably, and tell him the facts of life in the investment world. But now there are plenty of working mothers who can do it.

When I was a little kid making radio commercials, my mother took my earnings and invested them in a stock that we chose together. Then when I wanted a car to escape on weekends from my remote New England college, I sold my stock and combined the money with my earnings from all my summer jobs to buy that Volkswagen.

Then, when I was about twenty-five, my mother told me it was time I learned something more about investing, particularly in the stock market. And, she assured me, she wouldn't force me to deplete my pitiful savings. She would give me money. The only rule was that she approve the stockbroker and that she learn of my initial investments. After that, it was all up to me.

▲

A kid can feel great when a mother hands out grown-up power. And we all know money is power.

Marion, the funeral director, knew all about this. She sent her daughters to work during summers when they each turned thirteen. She paid for college, but told them, " 'Whatever money you make in the summer is what you have to live on during the year.' It encouraged them to get good jobs."

Marion knew something else, too. She was a divorced mother of two daughters. She'd seen many women stay in marriages "for whatever reason. They felt that they had to be protected. When I knew I had to get out of my marriage, I was glad I had the money to do it. Women have to have their own money.

"The day my daughter got married, I walked her down the aisle. I had raised her and paid every penny for that wedding. I looked at the woman priest ready to perform the service and the woman photographer ready to take the pictures. I turned to my daughter and said, 'If you don't want to go through with it, tell me now, and we'll turn around.' Fortunately, she's got the money and the confidence to do whatever she wants."

"My mother made sure I have some cash and some stocks," says her daughter. "My husband knows I have it, but he doesn't ask me about it. He has no idea how much I have. My mother always helped me choose investments. She looked out for us. I'm glad. I love my husband, but the divorce thing worries me."

▲

Since working mothers know money can make their children's lives a lot better, they often choose to give it to them while they're living, when they can see how their children and grandchildren benefit from it.

Bill's mother was a private investigator. She wasn't always a private investigator. Bill's father took her into the business because she could balance the books a lot better than he could. For tax and conflict-of-interest reasons, Bill's mother owned 100 percent of the business.

Bill had watched his mother in the business and enjoyed it. When he grew up, he joined her in it. They cooked up some good ideas together, got into industrial espionage and private investigations.

Bill's mom saw Bill was doing such a great job, she gave him 49 percent of the business. Then they found a buyer. And they divided the profits.

Now *that's* teaching your child the value of a dollar.

When they want to grow up to be like Mommy, it might be because she's making the best job offer.

▲

Line up the children who have grown up to do what their daddies do, and the line will reach to the moon and back a zillion times.

With mothers, the line will be much shorter. For the most part, their children have not stepped into their work shoes because there was no career to emulate.

For those who have been exposed to working mothers, there's plenty of evidence to show that they will grow up to do what their mommies do.

One day at the pediatrician, we were talking about working mothers, and the young medical student training with our doctor piped up, "My mother works."

"And what does she do?" I asked.

"She's a pediatrician," he answered.

At Amherst College a group of students called Amherst Women in Science assembled a panel entitled "My Mom the Scientist." Offering advice to the malleable young, the Amherst mothers on the panel were physicians, psychologists, and science professors.

Your children may not remember you for your pristine bathrooms, flaky pie crusts, and collection of needlepoint pillows, but they will remember you for helping steer them in the right professional direction.

As everything else involved in raising children, nobody says it's going to be easy.

First, there's a lot of wincing, grimacing, shrieking, whining, and complaining. Who wants to take *her* advice? Who wants to do what *she* says? Who wants to *be* her?

Yes, I went through all of it. I clearly remember grudgingly agreeing to go work for my mother, as if I were doing her a big favor. After all, it's tough to follow in your mother's footsteps. Is this what boys have gone through all these years in going into their fathers' professions and their fathers' businesses?

Having an achieving mother can make you want either to be president of the United States, to be better than she ever was, or to work alone in the basement of a university library cataloging doctoral theses for the rest of your life, to escape forever the possibility of a matchup.

It's nerve-wracking to think you'll never measure up to her professionally. It's hard to be introduced as her daughter when others have clear ideas of who she is, her levels of competency and authority, when you're a little pip-squeak.

The first day I worked for my mother was unbearable. I had to write a sixty-second radio commercial that I couldn't possibly compress to less than three minutes. I didn't understand, couldn't believe, that I could ever, ever, ever be as good as the worst copywriter there ever was, much less even close to my mother. At the end of the day, I walked into her office and burst into tears. "I can't do it," I blubbered.

"Close the door," she said.

"Kathy," she told me, "I never would have hired you if I didn't think you could do it. I know your work. I know how you think. I have absolute confidence in you. I don't want you to fail. I'm not going to be your boss. I'm not going to teach you how to write. You have somebody else to report to. I want you to believe you can do it." Then she told me the story of a famous woman in business who used to go home every night and cry when she first started working because she didn't think she could make it through the obstacle course. She rose to the occasion, my mother told me, and became a model businesswoman. I felt a lot better.

Isn't that just like a mother? And who's to say that's not how you're going to treat your children when they are ready for career advice? You'll be just like you are when they need help drinking out of a cup, tying their shoes, or tackling a term paper.

A mother is a mother is a mother.

My brother Rob learned this, too. He also went into the family advertising business, after a fling slapping up wallpaper and scrubbing exposed brick. Like me, he stayed in the business for a while. A while? How's fifteen years? Then he left to start his own marketing company, a pursuit well-suited to his personality. And now he's back working with his mother. This time, though, they function as independent contractors.

"I'm not working *for* her. We come up with projects together," says Rob. "She wants to get an idea and see it happen. She does the part she likes, and she lets me do what I do best. She really wants me to succeed.

"Before I make deals I run them by her to make sure I'm not giving the farm away. She's got a lot of business experience. It's hard to put a value on yourself. She tells me how to negotiate. It's nice to be able to call your mother. Because she's my mom, she's on my side."

▲

One thing children have to learn is that there's no escaping who you are. You're born with a certain personality, molded by your parents' interests. Somewhere heredity and environment mesh and, boom, there's you. So when you go to pick what you're going to do with your life, it's not a surprise to find your family in there calling to you.

Molly grew up with a mother who was very involved in what she was going to do with her life. Her mother had gone to nursing school, practiced nursing, and has evolved into an insurance-company executive. Her father never asked what she was going to do, but her mother told her, "You don't have to take my advice, but I'm your mother, and you could at least give me the courtesy of listening to what I have to say." What she said was law school. What Molly did was art history. Today, she's a museum curatorial assistant. There's a good reason for it.

"My grandmother was a museum curator," says Molly. "My mother idolized her and took me to the museum a lot. She was always enthusiastic about my interest in pursuing art history. She was just worried about how I would support myself, since her mother had quite a time of it.

"I didn't have that much contact with my grand-mother, but I can remember picking out a porcelain figure with her for my sister's birthday. Nanny was very particular about how it should be wrapped. I acquired that interest from her, and my family always knows when a present is beautifully wrapped that it comes from me. My mother always says, 'It's the artistic sensibility that Nanny passed on to you.'

"In college I intended to major in Latin and French, with no thought of art at all. But in my sophomore year, I had to figure out a fourth class to take. I took art history. It was the most interesting class that semester. I loved my professor and the subject. When I declared my interest to my mother, she fueled it with stories about Nanny. Like Nanny I give gallery talks and publish articles. My mother always says, 'Your grandmother would be so proud.' "

Pam always wanted to do what her mother did. Her mother was an actress, and when Mother's agent would call about an audition, Pam would always ask when he was going to send them both out on a mother/daughter audition.

"I thought it would be great to be in a television commercial together," says Pam. What could be cooler? One day her agent called and said, 'Okay, I have an audition for the two of you.' I was fourteen, and it was for Arrid Extra Dry. I had to say, 'My boyfriend likes me dry.' I was horrible. I was so nervous. I really had unconquerable stage fright. From then on, when I wanted to be involved with school plays, I was the stage manager or something. Now I'm a lawyer. Law is essentially like being on stage. Whenever I have to do a trial, I hold my breath and jump in. I must have gotten that courage from her."

▲

Some children do something else first before they feel the pull of the genes.

Jackie went off to college to major in psychology, but the thought of staying in school to get a Ph.D. was daunting. One day her mother, who had founded her own California produce business and became known as the woman who introduced and marketed the ubiquitous kiwi fruit, called and told Jackie that a business major was something she could use no matter what career she wanted to pursue. Jackie thought about it and agreed. During the summers, she had worked for her mother, going to the markets at two in the morning. Then, after college, she had two goals: traveling around the world and skiing. To get enough money, she went to work for Mom. Temporarily, she thought.

"After I took three years to travel and ski, I was ready to settle down. My father, who is a management consultant, asked me what I was going to do. I said I thought the produce business was exciting and that I wanted to work for Mom. That blew everyone away. Nobody thought I would go to work for her. I started as low man on the totem pole. I did what anyone in that position would do, and as I proved myself, I got opportunities. My older sister had already joined the company and had worked her way up to director of sales.

"Now I'm vice-president of the company, my sister is president. Sales have doubled since she's become president. My mother can't argue with success, but she's a real smart person. Sometimes she'll question what we're doing. As long as it makes sense, she has to agree.

"At this point, we can't do it without our mother. She's involved with sourcing and procurement and has very strong contacts. She still *is* this company. Everyone likes her. She loves to praise, never dwells on the negative. She has a way of dealing with people that is disarming. People trust her. She's always willing to take a chance. She points to her elbow when her intuition tells her something's a good idea.

"I try to emulate her ability to make people at ease. But I'm feisty. I get so impatient. I want to do something and go after it. She's calmer, tempers her anger. I really need to watch her for a while.

"She was ready for us to come into the business. She likes networking now and gets a lot of awards. She's reaping the benefits. We're here to take care of the business."

▲

Being in your mother's business can be the best or the worst thing in the world. Opportunities are tossed to the kid, who has to be deft enough to catch them and know which way to run with them.

Julie's mother is a financial consultant who manages multimillion-dollar accounts. When she took Julie in as her partner, they shared the work, but Julie says, "It took me a while to figure out I was accomplished. I wanted a lot of feedback. My mother doesn't sit around and rest on her laurels. She keeps going. She's on to the next piece of business.

"Around the office, she keeps her personal life to herself and makes sure everybody knows as little as possible. So people are afraid of her. They respect her, but they don't want to cross the line. Over the years, there have been rumors that she slept her way to success, that she was married to a broker who died, and she inherited the accounts. These things bothered her, but they didn't derail her. The numbers speak for themselves.

"I am more emotional. I come from a generation in which people speak their minds. I also cry easily. I tell everyone what I think. She cringes when I do it. She's reserved, diplomatic. She measures the moment before she says anything.

"When she plans meetings, she is perfect. I decided when I had to run a seminar for prospective investors, that I would do it just like she does. I sent out just the right invitation, had the right number of chairs, the right pencils and pads, the right refreshments. Then I followed up methodically. I was so proud of myself. She was beaming."

▲

Then, of course, there are those children who will go into their mothers' businesses, but will do it their own way, thank you.

Jim's mom and dad started a business together in the 1920s when Uncle Joe offered them his springwater business for $450. Dad went off at the crack of dawn to fill the bottles at a stream in the park, and Mom stayed at home to wash, sterilize, and cork the bottles before Dad loaded them onto his truck and delivered them. Mom did her work, the washing, the billing, the typing, and all, with five children underfoot.

"I enjoyed my children every day," says Jim's mother Sara. "I wanted us to have our own business because I wanted to be able to give it to my children one day. I knew they would never be laid off, and that they could make something for themselves. I made my daughters and sons help while they were growing up. The girls did typing, the boys loaded trucks. I didn't believe that teenagers should float around loose. I put them on the payroll, and I put half of their wages in the bank. Having all of that money would have tempted them to be foolish. But I'm glad I broke them in early. They liked working. Nobody ever fussed."

"Did she want her boys in that business!" says Jim. "When I was old enough to work full time, she went out and bought me a briefcase. She wanted me to wear a tie, to go out and represent the company. I sat in the park for a couple of days. Then I went home and said, 'Mom, here's the briefcase. I'm not going to be a salesman. Take me for what I am, or I'm leaving.' She had reached the point at which she didn't want to scare off her sons. So she accepted the fact that her baby was not a coat-and-tie salesman.

"By the time I came to the company, my parents were ready to give the business away. My dad sold it to me for a dollar, with the proviso that I would always take care of my parents. They left and told me where to send the checks. At the time their annual sales were forty-five thousand dollars. Now we're up to twenty million. My son and two daughters are in the business with me. He's president, one daughter is vice-president of sales and marketing, the other coordinates all the high-tech stuff.

"My mom is concerned that I gave up the reins too early. But I remind her she gave me the business when I was just twenty-one. My mother's in her nineties, and she still wants to know what's going on. We always took her to plant openings. She'd say, 'If your father were here—no, he *is* here, watching you and boring all the angels up in heaven.' She would burst into tears. What an ego trip for me. She's so proud."

▲

Some kids might have the talent to do what their mothers do, but not the temperament. In that case, everybody has to recognize the truth. Pushing will not make it so.

Lauren played the piano when she was young. No great surprise that she was talented. Her mother and grandmother were concert pianists. Her grandmother played in her native Germany, and even had sonatas dedicated to her by Clementi. She gave it up when she came to the United States. Lauren's mother played Carnegie Hall at the tender age of twenty-three. It was traumatic for her because of the horrendous stage fright she could never conquer. She gave it up, too.

Along came Lauren.

"My grandmother lived with us," says Lauren, "and she and my mother taught me piano. It was an overbearing aspect of my childhood. I was good, but they wouldn't let me just play for fun. My grandmother would shout from another room, 'That's supposed to be an F sharp!' My friend had a teacher who was training her to do recitals. I wanted a real coach like she had. So my mother sent me to a teacher, and he was disgusted with my so-called lack of dedication. I was crushed by this maniac. Today I won't play. If I'm at a party and sit down to play, people are shocked to see I know how. But, see, I'm embarrassed. I think I shouldn't play without tons of practicing beforehand. I quit before it killed me.

"My mother stayed in music. She became the conductor of the Chicago Chamber Music Orchestra. Then she started a choir and has kept it going for many, many years. She's also a professor at the University of Chicago. She's always had lots of commitments and been very serious about them. As ambitious as she's been for herself, she always wanted me to go my own way. She encouraged me to go into the city alone when I was growing up. It didn't ever bother her that I quit piano. 'Who would want that life?' she said to me.

"I'm in a different business, but still the arts. I'm a film publicist. I wanted my work to be fun and casual. I'm not in business to punch a time clock. I just want to work with intelligent, creative people. I don't push. I am very good at saying no when I don't want to work on something. But my mother is still pushing herself. In the last twenty years, she's taken up the cello. And she's always had a big rival who has irked her over the years. One night we saw her at a party, and my mother said, 'There she is, moving in on the important people.'

" 'Do you really care?' I asked her. 'She hasn't had the life you've had. She has no family, no children. Look what you have.' "

▲

A lot of people don't have the faintest idea they're living with a role model. Mother must realize, then, that everything she is doing just could be repeated in the future. The children might turn out to like it because you look as though you're enjoying it.

Kristin's mother didn't work when her three children were very little, but when they were in the elementary grades, she took a full-time job in the school they attended. Thirty-something years later, she is still teaching third grade.

And now, so is Kristin.

"I saw no value in teaching," says Kristin. "My mother thought it would be a good idea to get my teaching certificate 'just in case.' I said that if I taught it would only be at the college level and only in my level of expertise, whatever that meant. So I got a job in a model school at a university and taught five, six, and seven year olds. All right, I loved it.

"Now I am doing *exactly* what my mother did. I'm also in the same school as my two children. That situation used to cause my mother great pain. She would walk out into the hall during classes and see that my brother had been sent out of the room for misbehaving. She would slide him a book and say, 'At least be productive!' I have walked by my son who's been sent out in the hall to sit on the bench.

"I've had to teach my daughter, and on the days I was to teach her class, she would say, 'Don't wear that. Don't lean forward in your chair. Don't look at everybody with those big eyes. And don't call on me.'

"I talk to my mother about all of this, and she laughs. She encourages me to look on the bright side. I don't have to worry about how they're getting home from school, she reminds me. I really like her."

Children of working mothers know the value of working women.

▲

Expecting a child is a wonderful secret.

It's a thrill when you tell your parents.

A joy when you tell your little nieces and nephews.

An inspiration when you tell your friends.

And hell on wheels when you tell your boss.

Especially if your boss is a middle-aged man with three

children and a wife whose sole charge in life is to follow them around and cater to their every nose drip, diaper change, and puncture wound. The odds are better than even that this guy thinks working is not good for women or children.

When I was pregnant with my daughter, my bossman and I were having a discussion about some work I had done. He looked at me beatifically and said, "You know, there's nothing more beautiful in the world than a pregnant woman."

Heaven knows they can't *fire* you for having a baby, but they can certainly *ignore* you. They can forget to invite you to meetings. They can neglect to send you important memos. They can assume you didn't want to go to that boring old client dinner.

They can pressure you to tell them the exact moment the baby will enter earth's atmosphere. They can demand seven months in advance to know when you'll be going on maternity leave. They can be darned put out that the baby arrives early, when they'd counted on you to be sitting at your desk.

And they can be very, very, very sorry they just couldn't hold your mega-important job beyond the five-week maternity leave.

So why wouldn't working mothers-to-be feel guilty?

And why shouldn't you want to jump off a bridge when stay-at-home mothers glare at you, when your own mother questions your personal moral structure and your children's friends' mothers ask your children whether they feel like orphans?

Well, it's perfectly simple. These people just did not have working mothers.

They were not able to notice that their mothers did put those fine educations to work and would have totally lost it staying home all those years.

Surely, your brilliant children will not turn out to treat working mothers as moral black holes.

Because they have their own working mothers.

Granted, they may resent you now, may devise elaborate plots to humiliate you when you don't show up for the all-important class picnic, but when they grow up and go to work they'll understand.

In fact, they might find they like you a whole lot better when you work.

Stephanie grew up with a lot of conflicts about her mother's working. But her mother did not have the luxury of a choice. Her mother, a Holocaust survivor, came to the United States after the War with twenty-nine dollars. She took a job in California with a major airline, met a man while fixing his ticket, and married him. Once they had Stephanie, the airline wouldn't take her back because they didn't employ women with children. But she really had to work because she divorced her husband.

"We were stigmatized," says Stephanie, "because my mother was divorced and because she had this five-year-old coming home with a key around her neck. She was fired from one job because her boss said he could not tolerate the phone calls from me every afternoon to tell her I got home all right. When I was sick, she left me at home alone. I had chicken pox, and she called and told me when to take my oatmeal baths. At six I was dying because they rotated class mothers, and my mother couldn't do it. After school I would sit and wait for her. I had this feeling in the pit of my stomach when the kids in the neighborhood were called for dinner.

"But every year I won in my Brownie troop for selling more cookies than anybody else. She took them to her office and her friend's office. The other mothers were all fighting for the same blocks. I had a bigger territory. And I won the Barbie Dreamhouse.

"We moved to New York because she got a job in sales for a hospital-supply company. Their whole sales force was made up of women—fifty-five women—because the men who ran the company knew that women produce better sales. She was given the New York territory and did very well. By that time I was old enough to be alone when she traveled, and I loved it. The rules were that as long as I had my work done, I could have friends over. We were all very good. While my mother was in sales, she would rehearse her slide presentations to me. I was proud of her. She really made something of herself. She had a nice stock-option plan and made some money. For the first time, she was comfortable.

"Then I gave her the worst advice. I said, 'You know

what? Why don't you leave? You've worked so hard. You can always get involved in something else. Travel. Take it easy.' So she retired. She traveled to exotic places. She exercises like crazy. And now she spends time thinking about the most trivial things. I wish she still worked.

"After my daughter was born, she said, 'You better go back to work. If you don't, you'll go nuts.' She knows what she's talking about."

▲

Mothers who give up their jobs to stay at home to appease their guilt do not end up winning the Betty Crocker–June Cleaver Award. Many of them are wrecks, and it shows in their children.

Marnie was a high school teacher and a mother, and she took big hits from stay-at-home moms. "They used to gossip about how I left my children every day to go to work. I was teaching *their* children! I think that kids need a whole sphere in which they're not watched by their parents. It helps develop independence. Many of the mothers I saw put such pressure on their children. Sometimes it seemed they had nothing better to do than stand outside classroom doors peering into the windows to see if the teachers were doing their jobs. In the seventies, these women started getting careers. They opened boutiques, sold real estate. They were happier. So were their kids. I was proud of them. They deserve a lot of credit."

My mother was condemned for working, too. When my brother needed math tutoring, my mother took him to a woman math teacher in the neighborhood. One day when picking him up, my mother asked how he was doing, and the teacher said, "His only problem is having a working mother. If you were home helping him, he'd do just fine." Rather than answering that he wouldn't be any better in math if she stayed home, my mother turned on her heel and answered, "We won't be needing your services any more."

That's the way she's always handled abuse. She's not scared of it, and she taught me that. Once when I was working for her, a particularly dirty old client believed he had the right to give me and another young woman on his account a too-familiar pat every time we left his office. We ran to Mom. She wasted no time running to the client. She read him the riot act. He laughed her off until she said she was going to the chairman of his company. And I know she would have.

▲

When you have a working mother, you also learn the value of having a woman boss.

Alix is a physician who always worked for male doctors. "I had such a problem with my self-esteem with these men," she says. "I'd introduce myself as Dr. Walsh, and they'd reply, 'Hi, I'm Tom.'

"When I started working for a woman just three years older than I, my life changed. She has two young children as I do, and she understands the pressure. She called her kids one night to say she'd be home late, and the five-year-old hung up on her. This woman understands how much feedback I need. She's like a person stroking a cat's back. Suddenly, I'm ecstatically happy with my work. I'm doing what I went into medicine for.

"The way I'm talking about my boss is the way women who worked for my mother talked about her. To younger women who reminded her of her own children, she offered a lot of guidance. She was a mother figure. And always a dynamic force. Women always told me how lucky they were to work for her."

▲

People with working mothers can grow up to ask their mothers' business advice.

Mary Jane and her husband are attorneys, and when their son Tod graduated from law school, he told his parents he wanted to go on for an MBA, too. Mary Jane was a bit iffy about it.

"I told him he should talk to some people in the business he wanted to be in," she says, "and that I'd find people through my contacts. Tod had never experienced us not being supportive. Immediately, he didn't want to trade on the family name.

" 'Look,' I told him. 'All the name does is open a door. It doesn't get you a job. And because I know people is no reason not to talk to them. Learn the world of networking. And realize it starts with your mother.'

"I found somebody for him to see, and it turned out that two degrees was the right way to go. Now he's in Eastern Europe helping fledgling companies become private and capitalist. When they discovered Tod was a lawyer, they used him to negotiate contracts. I'm thrilled I could help. What's a mother for?"

When Annie started teaching little children, she turned to her mother, a former little-child teacher, to ask for advice. "She gave me lots of ideas. She told me to take in old clothes, have the kids dress up, and tell them how to say the items in French. When I wanted to work at her university, she gave me advice on playing the politics to get a job there.

"But the best advice I got from her was when I was in college. I needed to do an internship in juvenile delinquency for my degree in public policy. My mother helped make suggestions, talked with people at work, and made arrangements for me to have meetings with people over spring break. She called and told me to come home and work it out. I wanted to go to Florida with all my friends and accused her of trying to control my life. I couldn't see the big picture. I came home anyway. And now I can see it made sense.

"After college, I finally figured out she was my best friend. She's a rock who will always be there for me. I enjoy doing things with her. We have a philosophical connection. We're both involved, interested, and active. So it was nice when I knew that was my relationship."

▲

You know the expression about always asking a busy person if you want to get something done? That's how it works with working mothers. But it goes far beyond making sure shoes fit, beds are made, and braces are tightened on time. A mother has to find time to put some moral purpose into the lives of her children. A working mother who is out there seeing the world every day is in a position to know what's going on.

Irene worked hard, long hours, yet she showed her son and daughter the need "to have an ethical lifestyle with a sense of responsibility that shows that the world is bigger than I am. I wanted them to live an intellectually challenging life. I had to give them structure, a framework for living."

Her daughter Franny says, "My mother made me

aware of workers' rights because she was doing *pro bono* legal work for them. We were always boycotting things. The first time I saw iceberg lettuce in a restaurant, I said, 'What's this?' I had never eaten lettuce that wasn't bitter. Every time there's an election, I ask her who to vote for. How would I know from a list of twenty-five judges on the ballot who's the best? I definitely trust her judgment. She made me stand up for issues and causes.

"I discovered her influence when I was in elementary school. I saw a teacher hit a kid in the face with a ruler. I jumped up and yelled, 'Hey, you're not allowed to hit students here! That's illegal!' The class cheered me. I had become the spokesperson for kids' rights.

"I'm proud that I can stand up for what I believe in. I'm always labeled the feminist in a group. That's fine with me."

▲

Now what about those working mothers' sons who are now the middle-aged bosses? Some grew up to believe their wives were meant to work, to use their talents.

James was divorced from his wife of thirty years. "She was a talented person. She was a clothing designer. She shied away from getting involved in business. I wanted her to go into her own business. I think she would have been a lot happier. It wasn't until our youngest child went to college that she took a job in a bank. She likes working. I grew up thinking that people—men and women—shouldn't waste their talents."

▲

No kid on the planet wants his or her mother to be thinking of anything but me, me, me. That's how it goes. But some moms just get faint dealing with their kids all day. They sure do think about them, though, no matter what they're doing. Stepping on a plane you worry your kid will be an orphan by nightfall. Turning on the news you pray you won't hear that a school bus tumbled down a cliff. Getting cornered by your boss at 4:55, you hope you'll get to daycare before they file a missing-persons report on you with the cops. Mothers love like nobody else. They agonize uniquely. And whether they're around or not doesn't make all the difference.

What does make the difference, what does make growing up with a working mother positive is her perspective. As long as Mother lets her children know that they are the most important thing on earth, then they'll feel good about working mothers.

Good old Parker just seems to get it.

Parker is another of the sons of the woman who ran her own private investigation agency in Indianapolis. He remembers, "She was always there when the kids got home.

We never missed one thing from Cub Scouts to Little League. Business was always second to the family. We never really noticed she was working. She didn't want anybody to adjust. We didn't recognize what her contribution was. She was so subtle. Her personality and temperament never changed.

"Nobody ever said a hint of anything negative about her. She's always positive, sentimental, loving, and level-headed. She never had any reservations about hugging us three boys, no matter how old we got.

"All of us in the family got to see some discrimination and innuendo directed to her. Policemen and rough people used bad language in front of her. Because she was a woman, the decision might have been made not to include her in some of the cases. But she would probably have had good advice.

"She grew that company and always turned a profit, but she was never given the credit for it. My father didn't understand the money part, so he couldn't have praised her. Then, when my brother became her partner, he got the praise and respect.

"Still, though, when I'm offered a business deal, I talk to my mother about it. I think of her as a mom who happens to have a good business head. I know there are things I do differently in business because I am a man.

"But I see that anybody can succeed to any level."

You can't appreciate her until
you've taken a business call
while changing a diaper,
escaped from a meeting to get
to daycare before they
lock up, picked up clients in a
car filled with Cheerios dust, and
felt guilty at high school graduation
because you never helped out
in the art room even once and you
had thirteen years to do it.

▲

Maybe you know this story.

Maybe you *wrote* this story.

The nursery school is having a bake sale to raise
money to buy computers so that three-year-olds can learn
from a machine how to recognize letters and numbers so
they'll get into the gifted program in kindergarten. You, the

working mother who can write a multimillion-dollar grant proposal but can't bake your way out of a convection oven, open up your Julia Child at eleven on the night before the sweets are due. Discovering that you have the ingredients only for the most impossible, longest recipe in the book, you set about tackling it, down to toasting the damn hazelnuts. The next day you show up at school with your inspired confection, set it down on the table next to the other homemade yums the guilt-ridden working mothers baked in the middle of the night.

And then you see that the nonworking mothers have brought in boxes of stuff from the supermarket. You know, that junk food you won't let your kids eat. They bring it in for the bake sale. Without a whit of guilt.

There's no justice.

A working mother's life is crazy. It's making lists with things that are never crossed off. It's rushing. It's vowing to get organized. It's promising not to fall asleep in your daughter's bed when you're reading her a story.

It's wondering where your priorities are.

Sometimes you have to sit down and think about what your children are seeing. We didn't grow up with the ideas of mothers as whirling dervishes. They had a lot of stuff to do, maybe they complained every once in a while, or more, but they didn't convey the notion that life was out of control every waking moment.

I knew my mother was busy. But I only sort of knew

that she did all of the things she did. There was no sense that she was absolutely frizzled to the point of burning away to nothing. Of course, I was looking at her from my kid's self-absorbed point of view. I had no idea what she was talking about when she said she wanted to quit working. I never saw that she probably was frizzling until I was doing it myself.

Pam's mother is a singing and dancing actress who worked enthusiastically while Pam and her sister and brother were growing up. "When she was pregnant with me," says Pam, "she went to the obstetrician, explained what she did for a living, and asked if she could continue. He told her she could do anything she did regularly. A few days after her appointment, she was on *Your Show of Shows,* and she was singing and tap dancing on top of a huge drum, then jumped off into a split. The next morning she got a call from the doctor. 'What the hell were you doing?' he screamed.

" 'That's what I do,' she answered.

" 'Well, I didn't think you'd be dumb enough to do that!' he told her.

"Recently, my mother got some tapes of her old Ed Sullivan shows. She was tap dancing and singing at the same time and not even out of breath. There was no over-dubbing or the fancy video tricks they have now. I realized she was thirty-five years old and had three children. I'm amazed she could do that. I'm already falling apart with my first kid, and she was in incredible shape!"

▲

Smart mothers organize their lives, enlist the help of others, and structure their schedules to be able to be with their dear children and not make them feel as though they're on the list of chores.

Jo-Ellen has two young sons, and she has changed her schedule as a nursing supervisor so that she can be with them after school. "I don't feel guilty about not seeing them enough, but I do feel guilty when I'm rushing them. I feel bad that they have to hurry for my schedule. I should just let them be dawdling kids.

"My mother was chief dietician of a hospital, and she never seemed hassled and crazed as I am. When she worked every other weekend, my dad would do stuff with me. When she couldn't be home for lunch on weekdays, she or her boss would call and see what I was eating.

"Her life seemed easy, so I started out to major in home economics and dietetics, but I had to do a lot of the home ec stuff. Sitting down and doing intense, fine work drove me crazy. But my mother was a great seamstress. She did all that, too. I couldn't. I switched to nursing."

▲

Alot of mothers don't realize the commitment it takes to be a parent until the day dawns. Everybody's always telling you that, but it never seems to sink in. There's a new enthusiasm for the mother when it happens.

Alicia was in her residency program when her son was born. "My husband had a lot of expectations that I would take over the roles of his mother when we had a child. You know, she didn't work but ran the house and connected the family to the community. But it was hard to be a resident. I never understood how many hours it takes. My husband would bring the baby to the hospital so I could nurse him. I was in a chauvinistic hospital that said you have to want to be a physician more than anything. It just wasn't so. I quit the program. And I had to explain to my husband that I was raised in a more democratic way. Because my mother was teaching and wasn't home, we all had to take some responsibility. I learned from my mother that I had to put my foot down."

▲

Mothers have very clever coping mechanisms for handling stress.

Sally could not face the kitchen when she came home from work at night. So when her four children were old enough, she proposed that every child take a week of being responsible for dinner.

"I talked about menus with them," she says, "told them that if they made enough, we could have a dish Monday and Thursday, that sort of thing. I nixed anything too fancy. With one child, we ate her favorite spaghetti all week. Nobody complained. They all learned to be good cooks and enjoy cooking. It was a good plan."

Her son agrees. "She has half the cookbooks ever written, and I would pore over them looking for something. I loved to make Swedish meatballs from *The New York Times Cookbook*. My mother made me think I was the best cook in the world.

"And now I do a lot for my wife. Our schedules are different so we juggle who's shopping, who's cleaning, and who's picking up our son at daycare. I know my mother needed it."

▲

You hear all kinds of magazine and shrink talk these days about mothers as role models, with big heavy thoughts about what's going to happen to this generation of children who are raised by working mothers. Well, let's see. Maybe they'll learn how to do a billion things at once.

Ann's mother was an obstetrician-gynecologist and a single parent to Ann and her brother. "You know when you have those college applications and they ask you to write an essay about your role model?" asks Ann. "You're meant to pull some great luminary like Indira Ghandi or Eleanor Roosevelt. It's as if you live your life thinking you should be like someone you don't even know.

"My role model is my mother. I learned how to be a person by acting like she acted. I didn't have a role model that said stay home and wash dishes or do crafts. She was competent, strong in spirit and body. She was breadwinner, household manager, and baker of apple pies. I was never aware of her being stressed out. There was a real rhythm to her life.

"I learned that when you have a working mother, you have a better sense of all that women can do."

Denise always knew there was something special about her mother, but she never imagined she would see it in herself.

"My mother was always on the ball," says Denise. "Part of her is extremely young. She could juggle work and home. She did volunteer stuff. She treats every one of her plants like a child. And my dad didn't like to go out as much as she did, so she went to theater and ballet with friends.

"Now I hear the echo. I must be just like my mother. You're never aware of all you can do until you're faced with it. I learned to adjust as I add things on. And what I discovered from growing up is that it's important for kids not to be around only their mothers."

▲

Yes, it's formidable how much a working mother can get done. She can fold laundry with her left foot, feed the baby with her right hand, and cook a gourmet meal with what's left. So what does a working mother with time on her hands do?

Oh, remember maternity leave? Remember that time when you decided to work two days a week? Going to the market mushroomed into a three-hour ordeal. You were too bloody tired to take your kid for new sneakers. Laundry sprouted out of the hamper.

Carolyn knows what it's like. "I only work part-time now," she says, "and I'm absolutely disorganized. When I was working everything got done. I never knew how my mother did so much, how she was so organized. Now I see. She had to be."

▲

What about those nasty working mothers who are divorced and dare to sneak time away from their children to date? Are they ruining their sweet little bunnies? Probably not.

Stephanie's mother always had a man she was sort of seeing. "I was angry when I was younger," says Stephanie. "I wanted her to be with me. But she was young. She was twenty-two when I was born, thirty when she got divorced. Of course she had to go out. I was thirty-three when my first child was born. I had eleven more years of having no kids. I never saw this at the time. I realize it now."

▲

Of course, it's not only at home where the children of the working mother can appreciate her. They also see Mom as Working Woman. And they're able to gauge the future.

Lindsay's mother was an executive in New York with

a powerful position not often accorded to women in the 1950s. What's more, her parents were divorced, and her mother assumed many male responsibilities.

Lindsay says, "My mother worked for the same company for many, many years. Over that time, she was good politically. She rode out all the regimes. She was tough, astute, patient, tenacious. She knew when to play her cards. It wasn't until I was older, though, and going to work myself that I understood this. I was impressed that she had survived. I'm terrible at it.

"As a result, I chose not to have a high-powered anything. I work in my home. I can't do what she did. I can't be on top of everything. I need more time and space than she did. Otherwise, I don't think I'd be with my children enough. Not a day goes by that I don't remember my mother and all that she did. I appreciate her."

▲

Most children of working mothers have no idea what their mothers are up to all day long. So they try to make their mothers feel guilty about not being around. Not a tough thing to do. But the mothers have to buckle down. It's another one of those coping strategies that the kids can't value until much later.

Jean is an attorney, and when her now-grown daughter, Allison, was nine, she started calling from school that she was sick. "The first time, I dropped everything and picked her up," says Jean. "The second time I told her we were going to the pediatrician. Of course, nothing was wrong with her. I said, 'Allison, it seems to me you're playing a game. You're inconveniencing me. If the problem is that I'm working, you're going to have to know that I'm not giving up work. You have played this game to its full extent.' And she never did it again.

"Then she wanted to take piano lessons. It was hard for me to be on top of her to practice since I wasn't around after school. Lessons started getting harder, and she wanted to quit. I told her, 'We don't quit in the middle of the year just because something gets tough.' So she went on to take lessons for another five years. Today, she still plays for pleasure. I found that I always had to go right to the heart of the problem. I didn't have time for all kinds of behavior."

▲

Then, naturally, there are the kids who don't notice whether their mothers are around or not. Gary's mother left her law practice for several years while her three children were small. When she went back to work, she became a part-time partner.

"I always sensed she was a little guilty," says Gary, "but I was oblivious to the fact that most mothers were home and she was not. A cleaning lady let us in to our house. It wasn't a problem for me that she wasn't around, and it wasn't important that she be involved.

"My brother knew she was different. He had trouble. So she became a homeroom mother for him. Then when she did it for me, in turn, I couldn't figure out why she was wasting her time. I thought she was too busy with other things. I didn't feel the need to have her there.

"In junior high and high school she would meet with all my teachers. At the time I was almost a little embarrassed. It was her way of showing us she thought teachers and education were important. It must have sunk in to me. I went on for a masters and a Ph.D., and now I'm a college professor."

There's the daughter who never noticed her mother was working all those years while she was growing up. Ellen wrote articles and books and today is the chair of a commission in the New York City Department of Cultural Affairs. She always knocked herself out to get her work done, and made sure she could work at home so she could be available to her daughter after school.

Her daughter had no idea. When she went away to college and heard her friends talk about their mothers' big, high-powered jobs, she came home for vacation and said to her mother, "Why didn't you ever have a job? You'd be so much more interesting."

▲

I t's also nice for children to see that their working mothers are always women and always mothers. In other words, the moms don't turn off that nice, nurturing, emotional way they have about them.

Libby's mom was a cosmetics company executive who went back for an MBA when her children were teenagers. "When she went back to school, she would invite the people in her class, who were all men, to our house to study on Thursday nights," says Libby. "She served coffee and was kind of their social director.

"When I was thinking about a career, my father pushed me to go to medical school. He was very blunt and told me, 'You're smart enough to do it.'

"Maybe my mother was the softer person. She'd say, 'Are you happy doing this?'

"She was also into a lot of social causes. She is selfless. For people who have no one else, she'll take over. A woman in her apartment building became senile. The woman had no family, so my mother cooked for her, then helped the social worker get her into a retirement home. My mother visits her there. She also feeds people with AIDS, works for abortion rights and local politics.

"In certain ways, I can't measure up. I should be doing a lot more of this. She has given me something to strive to be."

Beyond working motherhood: something happens when you call her Grandma.

▲

It's hard to believe, but someday the pattering little feet will not belong to you.

You'll only borrow them from time to time.

When that day comes, you'll be the old lady buying hot fudge sundaes for the children twenty minutes before dinner.

And when they're completely revved up from sugar shock, you won't be the one who has to put them to bed.

If this seems all too gloriously far into the future, long past the time when you actually finish paying tuitions and sneaker bills, think about this.

Doesn't it seem like yesterday that you were in high school, an hour ago that you got your first job, and fifteen seconds ago that you were childless?

Thought so.

Then it's going to be any middle of the night now the phone rings with the news that you're a grandparent.

It won't be so bad.

For a working mother, in fact, becoming a grandmother could be bliss.

Because right now, which do you want to do when people tell you to enjoy your children while they're young? Throw up on their shoes or punch them in the nose?

Yes, yes, yes, you know all of this.

You *do* enjoy them. You *are* appreciating them, dammit. It's just that there's a lot a working mother has to squeeze in.

If it's your mother telling you this, simply tell her there is a reason that God created grandparents.

That's their job. They're supposed to enjoy your children every second.

Imagine, for a moment, being the grandparent. You get to be with the children when their hair is washed, they're nicely dressed, and they're on their best behavior.

You don't have any of the daily responsibilities and accompanying guilt of not performing at peak level.

Many working mothers come into their own when they become grandmothers.

I see it with my own mother. Now that she doesn't have to climb and scrape to build her business, she's more relaxed. She has the time to enjoy her family. The mothers of her generation I met were much less frenetic than the career-expanding mothers and fathers of my generation.

My mother is so content being a grandmother that she has turned it into a whole new career. She has incorporated the cute, touching, sweet, adorable stories of her nine grandchildren and others into books and newspaper and magazine columns.

Moreover, she's perfectly free to pursue this new career, spend as much time as she likes on it without having to worry about when the children need new toothbrushes and what the kids are going to have for dinner.

▲

Grandmotherhood is the time when the working mother can atone for her sins, and when the child who grew up with her walks around slack-jawed.

Patricia often complained about her mother's lack of direct involvement. "I never felt my mother was making sacrifices she wasn't one hundred percent willing to make," says Patricia. "She didn't compromise herself. She did not relax into motherhood. She loved her work, and I was a way station. It was like, 'I can't take you to Brownies, I have to compose a sonata.' I didn't think my interests were important enough for her. She didn't start enjoying me until I got older and we could discuss things.

"When I was in the hospital after delivering my first child, I saw an incredible transformation. She would have stepped over people with cleats to get to the baby. She was born to be a grandmother.

"There was such enthusiasm. I could see the same thing that happened with her job was going to happen with her grandchild."

▲

Grandmothers, too, have a way of understanding life and a knack for putting things into perspective that working mothers cannot jump-start into practice.

Sandra says, "I got a lecture last week that I'm too hard on my daughter. This is coming from the Queen of Nitpick. With me, she was a real Prussian. If I got a ninety-two on a test, she'd say, 'Great, but who got a hundred?'

"Now she's a super grandmother. She's understanding and forgiving. She has all the time and patience she never had for me."

And the grown-up daughters, as daughters often do,

have a better relationship with their mothers. They come to them for advice. But, again, just as they were as mothers, the grannies are not experts on sewing a straight seam. They're experts on putting the whole working/mothering/spousing thing together.

Michelle says, "My mother is an adoring grandmother, really good. All of the sudden, we talk to each other all of the time. She has great advice on being a mother and working. I'll say, 'I know you must have felt this way, didn't you?' Even though she's still working, she is much less exhausted. She has so much energy for my son."

▲

For some women, just having lived through the experience of having a working mother makes them never want to work full-time, though they know they have to do something. The reaction of the working grandmother to the situation is telling.

Janis is a writer and teacher, and when her son was born, "knew right away I didn't want to go back to work. I wanted to spend more time with my writing. There was no debate. But the women in my office looked askance at me. They thought I would be so bored staying home. I was doing exactly what I wanted to do, but I was worried about what my mother would think.

"My mother's life was very full. She sees that as positive. I don't. But when we went to visit my grandmother, who also worked all her life, it was my grandmother who looked at me disdainfully and said, 'Mothers should work.' My mother, the new grandmother, looked at me, looked at my son, and kept her mouth shut."

Margery came to a new realization after she became a working grandmother. She sees the current generation of young parents as better able to handle the stresses.

"After our children were grown, my husband and I would come home every night and watch the news. After about ten minutes, he'd say, 'What's for dinner?'

" 'I'm as tired as you,' I'd tell him. 'Maybe we should make dinner together.' It was a new, calmer reaction for me. Finally, I didn't feel put upon. When my children were growing up, I felt harried in most of my life. If I could have done it faster, I always thought, it would be better. And if it had always been the way it is now, I suppose I could have been the perfect mother.

"These days the fathers take a more active role. My son is totally supportive of his wife. He wasn't working for a while and did the shopping and cleaning. He does as much for his son as his wife does. He told me he felt jealous because he couldn't nurse the baby.

"I have so much more time for all the things I'm interested in now. I see my grandson a lot, but I have him over, he leaves, and I'm done."

The slower pace is nice for everybody. Including the grandchildren.

Jack's mother is retired, and she now has plenty of time for her grandchildren who are growing up with two working parents. "My mother always worked very hard," says Jack. "There are three of us boys. When my youngest brother was little, and there was no one to take care of him, she had to take him to the office with her. In perspective, I see it took tremendous effort.

"The grandchildren are growing up in these hectic households, so they like to hang out at her house more than home. Fine with her. Especially since she's finally got a granddaughter, the first girl in our family in several generations."

The children of working mothers I met were unanimous in their praise of their mothers as grandmothers. They loved the new time their mothers had to share. One mother promised to spend more time with her grandchildren than she had with her children. And since many still work, they're able to bring a whole new generation of children into their fascinating, vibrant worlds.

▲

There's one thing no grandmother ever forgets: she was a mother first. Often, it's not until the children of a working mother become parents that they really understand the deep roots of mother love.

Lisa had her ups and downs with her mother. "My

mother was always so busy. I thought she should have done more errands for me the way the other mothers did. She would never volunteer to chauffeur me around. She made sure dance classes and Girl Scouts were all within walking distance of our house. She was independent and thought I should be, too. The attitude was, 'Look, I could do it, so you could do it.'

"So I was more than a little surprised when I went into labor with my first child and my mother flew home in the middle of a business trip. Then after the baby was born, she waited on me. Waited on me! It was, 'Let me do this, let me make your breakfast, I'll draw your bath, I'll get your makeup.'

"I said to her, 'Having a kid makes me understand. You're *my mom* first. *Then* you're a grandmom.' "

**Working mothers develop instant
amnesia about how tough
it was to raise the kids.
It takes the children
a bit longer.**

▲

In the first place, mothers and children don't even remember the same things, much less remember them
the same way.

And in the second place, who's counting?

The children, that's who.

Only children would take note of every single blunder,

error, misstep, foul-up, indiscretion, blooper, and impropriety their mothers commit.

Mothers can't even remember the pain of childbirth. The proof of this is the fact that women continue to have children.

Who needs to remember the reason for every "I hate you, Mommy!" screamed by a three-year-old? As a matter of fact, my pediatrician told me not to take this ranting seriously.

"When the kid tells you he hates you," he said, "ask him how the weather is. Like the weather, the mood will change. It's only when your husband tells you he hates you that you have to worry."

If working mothers stopped to consider everything they do wrong in raising their children, they'd never get to the office. They'd curl up like little kittens and sleep on the windowsill all morning. Then what would the children say?

The truth is that a working mother doesn't have to have the cloud of guilt hanging over her head for the rest of her natural days. See the sunshine. Your children are going to remember mistakes no matter how long you breast-feed them, how much you cuddle them, how many flashcards you do with them, and how many Broadway shows you take them to. Yes, it's tougher for them to get over it. This is their childhood, after all, the source of their lifelong anxiety. You're an adult. You're through with all that.

You hope deep in your heart that if you love and adore your children, encourage them, nurture them, give them a code of ethics, and gently lick their wounds, they'll love you to bits and turn out okay. Despite you.

Lily taught while her children were growing up. As she puts it, "I was so busy I had no time to feel guilt or resentment that I was working. I never had time for anything. But I think the only thing in my family life that suffered was my cooking. My kids always ate fish sticks and French fries.

"My kids adapted to my working. My daughter was in a singing group and had to make her outfit. She didn't even come to me; she asked her friend's mother to make it. I don't think she was angry. She accepted that I was so busy. My son would raise his hand at the dinner table to get my attention. Then he'd pretend to fall asleep while I gave my answer. Maybe he was angry, but we laughed about it. One of my children was openly angry and hung out at a neighbor's house a lot. She took a lot of their values. I was sad about it, but I understood she wanted me to be like every other mother. She probably still holds it against me, but it didn't have lasting bad effects. I'm close with all of my children."

▲

Some working mothers who have to travel kill themselves to get home to go to every single school thing. But it's not always necessary.

Don's mother traveled a lot—about half her time was spent out of town as president of the League of Women Voters. Don says, "I can remember not wanting her to go out of town for an extended time once, and she sat me down and explained that what she was doing was important to a lot of other people. In short, she made me feel ashamed. I didn't ask again.

"When she missed soccer games, I was hurt. We resolved that problem together. It made me feel like a great martyr giving my mother up so that others could benefit. But she did go to soccer games when possible. She made a concerted effort to act 'motherly' when she could. I never had any problems beyond superficial anger.

"My dad really raised me. He fulfilled the traditional 'motherly' role as well as bringing home the bacon. He was incredibly supportive of my mother's work. I felt very proud of her. As I grew up, I recognized how poised she is. You can sense it even in a crowd.

"I was better because my mother worked. I was responsible at a much younger age than most of my peers, and that quality has remained with me."

▲

Mothers love to remember themselves as better than they were. No mother wants to think she was any worse than any other.

Eve laughs when she talks about what her mother remembers. Her mother was a sales representative and frequently was away on trips or out for dinner. "When she talks to me," says Eve, "she thinks she was home all the time. I remember night after night eating TV dinners. She thinks none of it happened. She remembers grand weekend trips. She'll often ask, 'Don't you remember going to see the horse at your uncle's farm all the time?' Yes, I remember going there *once*. She feels so guilty that she wasn't around, especially when she sees that I have chosen to work part-time so that I can be more accessible to my daughter. But, you know, I still respect my mother. She did a great job."

Some children figured out how to adjust so that they could handle their anger.

Lydia's mother was measured in the time she spent with her children. As Lydia sees it, "My mother had to be organized, disciplined, and careful with her time. She came home at six, we had to eat, she had to help with homework, the kids had to go to bed. If I wanted to tell her stuff, I didn't have the time. It drove me crazy. I had to talk loud and fast to get attention. It carried over to my adulthood. I never got anywhere with my clients. They thought I was shouting at them. I'm taking voice lessons and presentation skills classes to learn how to slow down. Also, I went into therapy so somebody would listen to my problems.

"When I told my mother about it, she cried. She thought it was a critique of her. I told her, 'I just want to be heard. I never thought I had a bad mother.' "

But, of course, the mother who doesn't listen to her kid because she's too busy can have disastrous effects.

Cynthia says her mother "always had time for others, for politics, for fund-raising, for her job. She didn't have time for me. The only way I could get attention was to do very, very well in school, and then it came to be expected. Now I get hurt when my husband is paying more attention to his family or friends than he is to me. If you feel your mother didn't spend enough time with you, you can have an overwhelming insecure side. I constantly think I wasn't good enough or smart enough or pretty enough."

▲

Achiever-type mothers loom large, and a kid must be strong to duck around them.

Lauren says, "I never felt I had as much energy as she did. Successful people seem to need about four hours of sleep. I have a frail constitution, and I go to a nutritionist.

My mother pops out of bed in the morning. She is contemptuous of people who suffer from headaches.

"Once when we were in Europe together, we *had* to go to every museum and cathedral. She ran through them like a checklist. Every day I would beg for mercy. Finally, she relented.

"I know the way I am, and I accept it. I would love to have a couple of months to walk barefoot on a beach and think about life. My mother? Never. She always says, 'Lauren, you talk to me about this and that, how you're running all your decisions through your mind. In my day, we didn't think about things. We just did them.'

"She is fearless. Successful people are. But I have gotten something important from her. I have her ability and her conviction to say no."

▲

Some kids develop real foresight about how to live their lives and raise their children by watching their working mothers. It's "I'm not going to raise *my* children like that." Well, whatever it takes.

Susan saw her mother come home from work at night so tired "she would flop in front of the television. It was the days before remote control, so she'd call upstairs, 'Susie, would you come down here and change the channel?' She was practically paralyzed.

"I knew I didn't want to work as hard as my mother. I'm a physician, and I got involved in rehabilitative medicine. It happens to have what I want. A schedule. I didn't seek out a place where they work too hard."

Susan's sister Molly says, "I wished my mother stayed at home. She must have had some funny little way of explaining why she didn't or brushing it off. But the days I would come home and had gotten an A on an exam or something, and she wasn't around or available at the office, I hated it. I wanted her attention, and there was intense competition for it.

"Now that I have a son, I want to keep working just as she did. I couldn't keep up the momentum with him if I didn't work. If I were home, all the other things like cleaning, laundry, and meals would have to get done, too. The time with my son is for having fun. Ideally, I'd like a schedule that's full-time but flexible.

"If I didn't work, it would put pressure on my marriage. I would look to my husband to provide more of the things I strive for myself in my job. A risk to giving up my job is that I wouldn't want him to feel he's not interested in continuing the relationship but thinking, 'How can I leave? How would she support herself?' Now I understand the reasons my mother always worked."

They never felt distant from Judy, their mother, though, perhaps because her mother worked, too. Judy says, "I always wanted more closeness with my mother. There were five kids in my family, and when I'd tell her I wanted to be closer, she'd say, 'My children are like the five fingers of my hand. How could I love one more?'

"I felt the same thing from one of my daughters once on vacation. She came running out of the ocean to the towel where I was sitting alone on the beach. 'Mom,' she asked, 'don't you wish you only had one kid and it was me?' I knew exactly how she felt. I was determined to stay close with my children no matter what."

Today, they're spread around a bit, but they stay in close touch.

▲

Now somebody's got to have long-lasting anguish, right? There has to be at least one out there who is still suffering from the fact that Mommy was not there with milk straight from the cow and cookies warm from the oven when Baby Darling came home from school. Yes, you mothers of sons, beware. The boys seem to take it pretty hard. You can see it in their wives.

Andrew is executive producer of a prime-time television network news program. His mother is French and always knew she would work, which has always been a common bit of understanding for cosmopolitan European women. She moved to the United States and became chief of the French Interpretation Section of the United Nations. She and her husband raised their two sons in the suburbs of New York City. Andrew missed his mother being around. He says, "I would have liked a closer family. I grew up very independent—for better or worse." Today, his wife works, "at home, as a mother," caring for their three children. Andrew and his family appeared in an issue of *Fortune* with the screaming headline, "CAN YOUR CAREER HURT YOUR KIDS?" Plunked in the middle of guilt-baiters about malaise, depression, and nonattachment of young children is Andrew's family, illustrating "an increasingly rare breed. Andrew earns enough . . . to allow his wife to stay home with their three kids."

Tom's mother was a psychiatrist and was not readily accessible to him. A staff of servants looked to his needs. "I don't suppose my mother was distant from the children," says Tom. "If there was something we needed, we could call her on the intercom."

In contrast, he married a woman who "came from a Beaver Cleaver house. She was my idyllic notion of what people were like in the suburbs. She is fairly intellectual with literary and artistic interests." Since they've been married, she's gone back to school to get a graduate degree in linguistics, but she's never put it to use. She's had part-time secretarial jobs and "didn't want to work in what she was trained in. And she never wanted to teach," says Tom. "I have mixed feelings. I don't like the idea where both parents work full-time and daycare is the social life. Why do people have children to begin with? On the other hand, for the mother not to work at all is probably not a great idea either. It's nice to have something else you're interested in. My wife's just not sure about her career."

Kip's mother ran her own business. He says, "I think happy and well-adjusted offspring of career mothers are the exceptions. Being the father of two young children I have come to realize the crucial importance of proper parenting. I am convinced this requires the presence and attention of at least one parent, male or female, *full-time!*

"The payoffs and consequences of absent parenting must be weighed heavily. Alienation, loneliness, drug use, and teenage suicide are stiff prices to pay for that third car in the garage.

"We have unconsciously debased the status of the parenting mother, I think, and that is a cruel thing to do the women of this country who have chosen this path."

See what I mean?

▲

On the lighter side, how about lunch? Lunch-making is a symbol of all that mothers are supposed to do. Feeding, wrapping, packaging, sending off. Lovingly. For some kids, lunch became the focus of resentment. These kids didn't miss their mothers, exactly, but they missed that motherly aspect.

Ann says, "My mother was a doctor and worked very hard. She was a good mother, but she didn't have a lot to give. That's just how she was. She never realized lunch seemed a nature of caring. She was too busy to pack my lunch—it was just lunch, after all—and I missed it. I ate the school lunch. So for my son I make the kinds of lunches I never had. I put in a lot of little containers and wrapped things. I'm busy, too, but it seems I'm giving him something of myself during the day when I'm at work."

Rachel wished her mother made her lunches, too. "My mother didn't even make breakfast," says Rachel. "Either one of my parents could have gotten up in the morning and done this. I rebelled and wouldn't eat it, but I *would* put an empty bowl and spoon in the sink. Fortunately, my brother ate enough cereal to make it look like we had both eaten.

"My brother taught me to make sandwiches for lunch. I wanted a spiffy lunch. I wanted someone to make me a tuna sandwich with lettuce and tomato, pack a bag of grapes and carrot sticks. Of course, it was too much trouble for me. But I'd always pack an apple because I figured a mother would pack fruit, then I'd throw it out at school.

"I hated having to do so many things for myself. I bathed myself, washed my own hair. It wasn't that I wanted my mother to do the shampooing for me, but I wanted *someone*.

"My mother seemed to have all kinds of time for everybody else. When I was in medical school, I begged to live at home with my parents so I could save money. My mother said no. 'But you put up the world. Why not me?' I wanted to know. In the long run, of course, she was right. It would have driven me crazy. It was another way she pushed me out to be independent. I never wanted it, but I did it. I don't suppose it really mattered."

Her mother, Miriam, says, "Fortunately, I had the energy level to do what I wanted to do. And I wanted to do all of it. I worked, I volunteered, I ran for office. So, naturally, I was eager to watch my kids get independent. I wanted my kids to learn to do their own stuff. I figured lunches they made themselves they would be more likely to eat. I never made breakfast except for Sunday brunch. My daughter swears I gave it up when her brother went away to college, but it's not true. Once, though, I made breakfast when my son was home from college. He said, 'Mom, are you trying to tell me you have a terminal illness?'

" 'No, just trying to tell you I'm an unpredictable mother.'

"You have to give kids freedom when they know how to use it. I sent my children on public transportation very early. I never told them not to do something. I encouraged them. I trusted them. I've always told them, 'As long as there's a phone and a plane, you can live anywhere you want in the world.' The ties are not physical or spatial. They're spiritual."

And what does Miriam's mother say? Well, her mother also worked. She had wanted to be a doctor, but never had the money to go to medical school. Instead, she became involved in education. Naturally, she doesn't remember that her daughter might have had it hard because she wasn't home. Though Miriam calls her mother "a remarkable woman, inspirational," she still leaned over to Miriam at a grandchild's graduation and said, "I have to hand it to you, Miriam. All this work and no contact with them. I had my doubts. But you could leave these children on a desert island, and it wouldn't be a desert much longer. They each have a strong sense of self, a lot of empathy, and an understanding of responsibility.

"I didn't know how this would work out. But I see how wonderful the children are."

As my mother always says, "Don't get so involved in the duties of your life and your children that you forget the pleasure. Remember why you had children."

▲

Just as sure as the day dawns when you have to tell your unblemished, guileless children that there is no Santa Claus, Easter Bunny, Chanukah Charlie, or Tooth Fairy, so, too, will you have to look yourself in the eye one day and say, "Honey, there is no Supermom."

Because no matter how many degrees you have, how

many courses you've taken in child psychology, or how much experience you have, you just can't juggle flaming clubs for twenty-one years straight. It's too dangerous. Something will catch on fire and explode. Don't try this at home.

But it's hard to see the truth of the matter when you're in the middle of it. Yes, you want to be with your kids when they're small. But what happens to your career? Is somebody going to crash through the glass ceiling faster than you do? And what does your husband say after you've been playing Chutes and Ladders all night and then end up collapsing onto your side of the bed with your pantyhose still on?

Worst of all, just how are you going to feel about yourself when you realize you can't do it all—perfectly?

Jane Pauley says, "Say goodbye to a social life, because you can't have a family life, a professional life, and a social life. I think you're allowed to have two, but you can't have all three."

True, many mothers find it easiest to give up the social life. As Caroline says about her divorced mother, "The price she paid for a successful career was no love life and no vacations."

And Lucy's divorced mother, who was an obstetrician, "never went out. It made me sad to see her sleeping on the couch in her clothes because she knew someone was going into labor."

Marion, the funeral director, worked constantly, could

never plan for any personal moments other than Saturday nights, and told her children, "The only things you're forbidden to do are become funeral directors or ride a skateboard."

But there's nothing like perspective. Listen to the working mothers with grown children.

Elise edits an alumni publication of a large university. She has four children, plus grandchildren, and she's still working. "Initially, I wanted to go to medical school," she says, "but I was discouraged by the two universities where I wanted to apply. So my expectations for my career were not enormous. Now you must have a graduate degree, but not thirty-five years ago when I started. If I started working now, I would think about climbing up the ladder.

"Having it all was not a concern for me. I didn't aspire to be a CEO. There was no doubt I wanted a family. And because birth control wasn't as sure a thing as it is now, I had them very close together. If I'd been thinking about it, I wouldn't have done that.

"Working seemed a natural thing for me. I was interested in too many things to stay home. I never thought of my family as an interference. I wanted them. When I had to make cupcakes, for example, I was simply inconvenienced. I always felt I was rushing.

"I benefited at work from raising a family and running a household. I learned how to do ten things at once and how to establish priorities. I have to have things organized.

"I was a strict disciplinarian and tried to keep a tight rein on my children. I made them understand why they had to call home when they went someplace. I had to make the teenage problem easier for myself because I wasn't really there. My children did take advantage sometimes. One day when I was getting dressed for work, I got a call from my daughter's hockey coach telling me my daughter was not at school. I called my office and said I had a family emergency. By the time my daughter came home that afternoon, the school and the police were out looking for her. It turned out she had played hooky with a friend. I figured that facing her teachers with the truth was enough punishment for her. I know that each of my kids tried pot, but they never got into trouble with it. I think all of this was experimental.

"They have all turned into such wonderful adults— one is a marvelous parent. We're all close. They've learned the value of friendships. They still have their high school friends. And my three daughters all grew up with the idea that boys can be friends. For me, they were always potential dates. I have learned a lot from my children. When they were growing up, they did chores to earn their allowances. My son was the first to be asked to take out the trash. The girls said I was sexist and that he could wash the dishes, just as they did.

"I took time for my children. They were always the most important thing to me. We're all better people for it."

▲

Many of the mothers from this Old-Mother-New-Grandmother Generation went to work with plenty of mom role models, but very few working-mother role models. Sure, there was Eleanor Roosevelt, who even wrote an essay, "Should Wives Work?" in which she encouraged women who would be unfulfilled doing little more than raising children, changing curtains, and caring for and feeding their husbands' careers to get out of the house and into some kind of work. But let's face it. How many of us can be Eleanor Roosevelt? She's an inspiration, but a role model?

These days a lot of these moms are asked to speak to younger working mothers in their fields to tell them how they did it. How they emerged as living, breathing humans with relatively happy children.

One of these women is my mother, who says now that she might have looked as though she was doing it all comfortably, competently, but she was spinning inside. To keep her spin to a manageable pace, she made sure she had plenty of help at home and that she was able to delegate at work. She never held herself up as the only one who could do everything. In that way, she was able to shine at what she did best.

Another of these experts is Florence, who started her

career as an attorney before her children were born. "My life is such a parody of conventional wisdom," she says. "I got a job in the fifties in a major law firm in my city. I told them, 'I am going to leave when I have children.' They understood that I had limited expectations. In those days men liked women who expressed a desire to take care of children.

"I stayed there for a couple of years, until I was pregnant with my first child. Then I left and had two more pretty quickly. I never intended to go back until my kids were older. Plus, my husband had a working mother and hated it. He made me promise I would stay home with the kids. It was okay with me.

"When I wasn't working officially, I did a lot on the side. I became active in the Bar Association, wrote an occasional will, wrote appellate briefs, and made a lot of contacts. Actually, staying home helped my career. I did a lot of *pro bono* work, and that gives you status and stature in the legal community.

"My kids were grateful that I stayed home. I was always there for them. I was at every play or teacher conference. Then I got involved in a parent-school group. Our family was child-oriented. My husband was a physician, but had a hospital-based practice so that he would be free to be with the children.

"When my youngest child was in first grade, I decided to go back to work. I had no commitment from my firm, of course, but one night at a cocktail party my husband asked a partner from my old firm, 'Do you know anyplace that would take her back?' The partner announced, 'We will!'

"So after nine years, I went back three days a week. It was at a point where it didn't make a difference to my children. Now I wanted to be a partner. It became a matter of pride. Imagine in those days a woman asking to be a part-time partner. They let me do it.

"I had to defend myself about having a career. Mostly men, sometimes women, asked, 'Don't you think your children will suffer?' Of course not. I always put them before my career.

"Motherhood is the most fundamental instinct there is. Nothing is more feminist than having children. Women are different from men, and they should recognize it, celebrate it. Women should have the choice to have children and a career. They shouldn't be deprived of it. Employers must be more flexible.

"I always thought the fact that I had something to go back to gave me confidence. I could never have stayed home forever. I was home with the kids because I wanted to be. I had higher self-esteem than many of the college-educated mothers who were staying home. Many mothers now think staying home is a betrayal of their education. That's very sad.

"My life suited me perfectly. I wouldn't criticize someone who did it. My children are all wonderful. But my career was a matter of happenstance, good luck, and training. Law is the perfect career if you want to take time off.

You can always look up new laws. The fundamentals and techniques don't change as they might in medicine or high technology.

"I feel sorry for the young women lawyers today who feel such pressure to do everything. I tell them that if you can't balance career and children, don't try. Your children deserve the most you can give them. You can't have everything. Nobody gets everything they want out of life, but you don't have to eat gourmet banquets every night. It's better to have more quality time in your life than less. My advice is to stay home with your kids while they're young. Taking time off can work out okay.

"But also leave a little time to enjoy life. I made sure I had moments to myself. My family knew when my quiet times were, and they had to respect them.

"Women have a lot to do. We have to be stronger, brighter, and better than men. Fortunately, that's not difficult."

▲

Now my mother, who's a champion at coming through with advice, solicited or not, says, "The more things there are in your life, the better for everybody around you. You're a more interesting person to yourself, your husband, your children. It's not only the woman who goes to the office, but the woman who does volunteer work, who goes back to school, who stays aware of the world around her."

Again, she says, "Don't get so involved in the duties of your life and your children that you forget the pleasure. Remember why you had children."

And that's what Nadine's mother has rediscovered. For while her children were growing up, she was so busy, so exhausted, that she came home at night, "sat on the couch, snapped on the TV, and shouted, 'Where's my newspaper?' " says Nadine. "She didn't take time to take care of the family. My father took charge of everything. She never had time to decorate the house. She couldn't even follow the news. She was never a listener, always a manager."

Then her mother retired. And what Nadine has discovered is the love that was always buried under the pressures of the job. Now that she's grown up and has her own wild, pressured life, she sees her mother's love differently. She's learning what's important.

"My mother's not really doing anything," says Nadine. "She's unwinding. She's turned into a different person. It's like having a mother for the first time. It's the most amazing transformation. She's so mellow.

"She's asking questions. She finally wants to talk. She always had so many things to worry about with her job. She never wanted to hear about anything that didn't have something to do with work. Now she listens when you talk, and she smiles. She pays attention to what's going on in the world.

"She uses her administrative skills to settle disputes in the family. She negotiated a fight I had with my father. 'Your father really loves you. He actually meant to say this,' she told me. She stopped the fight. It's like a different person has moved into the house.

"She's totally happy. The tension level in the house has dropped incredibly. I wish she'd retired a long time ago. It makes me realize how much a kid's life is built around the stresses of the parents.

"She planned a big seventieth birthday party for my father. She had it catered because that's her style, but she never would have done this before. My parents went on a cruise, and she wrote me ten-page letters about her feelings. Before, all I got were thank-you notes: 'Dear Nadine, Thank you for the gift. Love, Mom.'

"She's fixing up the house. I saw her putting on switch-plate covers. There never were any."

And her mother, who is in the middle of a visit with her daughter because she just became grandmother to Nadine's newborn son says, "I never missed anything when my kids were young because I was too busy to know what I was missing. I loved my work. So when I retired I got involved in other things. I thought I would write. If my daughters can write, so can I. I've been volunteering for the organizations I always wanted to work with."

She passes the hungry infant back to his mother and says, "I've been here two weeks, doing laundry ten times a day and driving my daughter and her husband crazy because I still like to give orders. If she had had the baby while I was working, I might have taken a two-week vacation to be with her, but I would have been calling the office several times a day. Something would have been going on.

"You know what? I *love* not working after all these years. The best part about not working is getting to know your children and husband again. If anybody's a saint, it's my husband. Since I've been visiting Nadine, I've missed him. For the first time."

Her husband, who has been listening to the whole conversation, comes up behind her, puts his head on her shoulder, and softly sings, "Getting to know you . . ."

And on the sofa, Nadine is discussing her immediate future. "I hired a full-time housekeeper/*mamacita* because I'm going back to work in two weeks. I'm also writing a book that's due in March. And my art is really starting to take off."

She laughs. "I don't have the vaguest idea how I'm going to do all these things."

Sure she does.

Afterword

Working mothers will get their reward.
They just don't know when.

▲

et me introduce myself.

I am the other mother in this book, the mother of the mother who wrote it. In case you wonder what I am doing at the end of the story, I will tell you.

Diane Reverand, my daughter's editor, sent Kathy a fax one day and wondered, "Would you like to ask your mother to write a chapter, or is that a daughter's worst nightmare?"

My reward is that my daughter thought it was a fine idea, and so began my thinking about the rewards of being a working mother and when and how our children begin the latter-day payoffs that make earlier troubles fade.

I am the first to admit that our life has not been all chocolate sodas and trips to the zoo. Indeed, I have spent many days and nights assuming that there were no rewards, only regrets, in being a working mother. There were times that I thought my children were lying awake at night trying to find ways to bedevil me because I wasn't there with them twenty-five hours a day.

What hurt and upset me for so many years?

Well, try a few of these for size; they may fit in your household, too. I was filled with remorse

. . . when my son told me he'd never let his wife work (and didn't).

. . . when my daughter didn't act as if it was special when I was a homeroom mother, a PTA officer, and a Brownie leader.

. . . when my son scarcely noted my presence at soccer games and tennis matches—even though I'd bolted lunches, skipped meetings, and driven like a maniac to be there.

. . . when my daughter didn't confide her reasons for teenage sullenness, anger, and outrage and let me assume it was always my fault.

The rewards began to come as my children grew older.

Perhaps their anger subsided—anger at the world and at me and at themselves as we all matured. I often wonder if it was a single event or group of events.

Did they relent when they went into the same or an allied business as I?

Did it happen when each of them married successfully?

Was the beginning of their understanding the births of their children and the realization that parenting wasn't as easy as they assumed it to be?

Perhaps it is all of the above.

These days I find that I am rewarded regularly. I have an inner satisfaction and joy

. . . when my son's daughter says she wants to be a writer "like Grandma."

. . . when my son uses me as a business advisor and not just as an advising mom.

. . . when my daughter convinces me that she really does want me to write in her book.

. . . when my son agrees to let his wife "work if she wants" on a flexible schedule now and more as the children get older.

. . . and, most of all, when both children turned out to be participating parents with recollections of a happy childhood.

Now, from my present vantage as a working mother's working mother, I feel qualified to advise mothers just starting the path I trod so long, so I have put together some thoughts that may reduce the level of perpetual anxiety that seems to plague every mother who works outside the home:

1. Don't expect your children to be better than other people's children in order to prove that working is okay.
2. Remember that you don't have to be perfect in everything.
3. Trust yourself and your children to do what's right for your relationship in the long run; meanwhile, accept the truth that everybody has some bad days, bad months, bad years.
4. Never forget that independence is a gift, not a burden, for your children and that you are giving them a role model of a caring, independent person.
5. Don't apologize for working.
6. If you want to complain, talk to yourself—no one else really is interested.
7. Make things fun every time that you can.
8. Teach responsibility. Don't do everything for your kids because you're not there to do some things.
9. Don't let so-called friends and do-gooders do bad things to your psyche. Doom dealers and naysayers have always been with us; working moms didn't invent them.
10. Above all, when time runs out and the days get

short, let the beds go unmade and dishes un-
washed—but do stop to realize how much you
truly love each other, no matter how many mistakes you both make.

Lois Wyse,
September 1992

ABOUT THE AUTHOR

KATHERINE GOLDMAN is the working mother of two small children. She is the daughter of a working mother, Lois Wyse, who is an advertising executive and best-selling author. Katherine is married to Henry Goldman, a reporter with *The Philadelphia Inquirer*. They live in Philadelphia.